A Constellation of Connections
Contemplative Relationships

By Vanessa F. Hurst, MS

Illustrated by Merlin T. Lee

Wildefyr Press
Louisville, KY

Wildefyr Press
Louisville, KY 40242

© 2016 Vanessa F. Hurst

Published in 2016
Printed in the USA

ISBN-10: 0-9908091-2-9
ISBN-13: 978-0-9908091-2-8

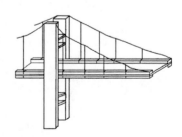

Thanks to my constellation of connections:
Merlin, illustrator and layout artist;
Michelle, contemplative spirit and mindful beta reader;
and Karen, wise woman and stellar editor.

After writing this book, I now realize that "I haven't failed, I can tell you 10,000 ways not to be in relationship." (Building upon the Thomas Edison quote: "I haven't failed, I can tell you 10,000 ways not to create a light bulb.) So, thanks to all my relationship partners. Each one of you has helped me to learn how to be in relationship.

Table of Contents

Introduction

The first time that I really thought how important and life altering living in relationship happened when a friend of mind traded an astrological natal chart for a Second Degree Reiki attunement. Imagine my surprise and consternation when I learned that my life lesson was about relationships. This discovery happened when I was in my later thirties and had a series of failed relationships; the last one culminated in a divorce. My initial fear-filled thought was "What happens when I don't get this right? Will this life be in vain?" Looking back, I see how narrow my understanding of relationship was.

Flash forward almost ten years. I moved to Louisville, Kentucky, after accepting a position at The Merton Institute for Contemplative Living. There I found another way of looking at relationship. The Institute's definition of contemplative living resonated with me—I live contemplatively while in relationship with my self, the Sacred, others, and all of creation. In that epiphany moment, I woke to the realization that relationship is less about romance and all about connection.

I would be remiss if I didn't mention the impact that Thomas Merton has had on the whole of my life. Through my interpretation of his writings, my understanding of relationship has deepened. Prior to my move to Louisville, I had integrated the writings of Starhawk, Dorothy Day, Lao Tzu, Rachel Carson, Pema Chödrön, and many others into my lived experience. Thomas Merton's writings were the catalyst for understanding how to live in deep relationship. Through comparing and contrasting his writings with the works of my other teachers, I more clearly saw and understood the invisible strands that connect us in relationship.

What I share about my understanding of relationships is based on an amalgamation of the teachings of spiritual masters who shared with the world both secularly and spiritually. Through them, I see relationships not as two individuals flowing in and out of connection in unaware ways, but as a way of interacting and connecting intimately with others on our life path. These connections may be fleeting, for a lifetime, or somewhere in between. As I reflect upon my more successful relationships, I discover they had, to some degree, three components: silence, compassion, and communion.

I began to visualize relationships as a constellation of connections against the backdrop of a dark night sky. Silence creates the inky darkness of the canvas. Within silence we create and sustain relationship. Each of our essences is represented by a twinkle in the night sky. Each spark is fueled by compassion given and received. Thriving relationships connect us to others through communication that transcends the ordinary. Communion connects us to others in our constellation of connections.

For me, relationship is only possible, only accessible, through a night sky consisting of the key elements of silence, compassion, and communion. If this way of relationship resonates with you, may you paint a glorious night sky filled with many connections of clarity and understanding.

Vanessa F. Hurst

Chapter 1

A Constellation of Connections

Upon our life canvas we paint a glorious night sky that is unique to each of us. In the array of stars, we are Polaris, the North Star of our sky. Each person, each part of creation is a star twinkling against the indigo backdrop. Here in the inky darkness of our night sky, we connect to others in relationship. These connections create a vibrant, dynamic constellation. Each interaction, no matter the duration, impacts and influences our constellation of connections.

Through our awareness of these connections and our interactions with others, we create the dynamic matrix of our life. Within relationship our constellation glows, and we live deeply, fully, and vibrantly. These connections invite us into a greater understanding of our self and are vehicles through which we live our life purpose. Through relationships, we evolve and transform.

Within every moment of life exists the opportunity to connect and forge relationships in both the natural and human-created world. Perhaps we discover a way to more deeply understand our self or strengthen our connection to the Sacred. Our connection with another may continue or even strengthen in the same vein. It may shift into an entirely different way of connecting. Each relationship represents a thread in the interconnected and interdependent web that is our constellation.

Throughout my life I have had great difficulty in letting relationships transition into a different way of connecting. When I moved to Louisville, my relationship with a very good friend began to change. Instead of becoming closer because we lived closer to one another, our relationship became strained. On several occasions we attempted to revive the relationship, but we could not. We drifted from close friends to acquaintances. The eventual transition was both painful and difficult. Although the relationship would have shifted, with honest communication the evolution would have been less angst-producing.

Relationships help us maintain a delicate balance between complacency and full-throttle living. We may find our self being focused on the relationship and doing all possible to be present to the other, while at other times we may find our self merely being physically present but not having a mentally, spiritually, or emotionally supportive relationship. This balancing act requires awareness and response.

Through awareness we discover the lessons and challenges offered by a specific relationship. When a relationship shifts in ways that cause us to drift away from another, we may become angry or blame the other or the situation for the change. Only when we reflect upon the relationship do we fully understand the life challenges.

When the close relationship I spoke about ended, I had an opportunity to acknowledge that assuming a "helper" role in relationships was not a better course for me. This relationship taught me to be aware of why I was connecting with others. With this awareness, I could choose individuals who wanted to be with me instead of those who needed something from me.

Some interactions trigger rapid changes in relationship partners. We may experience growth in fits and starts in some, while others may nudge us in quiet and gentle ways. Our life is spent in relationship with our self, others, the Sacred, and all of creation; only in relationship are life challenges revealed and successfully met. Relationships are the arena of our life. Without them, we would stagnate.

We meet life challenges when we are our best authentic self. Staying in the aforementioned relationship would have stunted each of our abilities for growth. Leaving, though painful, allowed

[handwritten margin note: Something I need to really work on emotionally/draining] [scribble]

— Nash

me to reflect on the potential for growth and to make changes. Through relationship we embrace our life purpose and open our eyes to the extraordinary — those parts of our reality that reveal the sacred and connect us to the world in profound ways.

When we live intentionally in this constellation of community, we live in awareness of the vibrant, organic nature of life. We recognize that life is not static. It may appear that we choose to connect in seemingly random ways, but there is little that is random in our life. Everything and everyone stimulate growth. Through these connections we empower others to live in the wonder and meet the challenges in their lives.

Each star in our constellation represents a person, the Sacred, or a part of creation with which we connect. The Sacred is present in each component of the sky. It is present in the indigo blue of the night sky and in the twinkling light of each star. When we enter into and sustain a relationship with the awareness of the ever-present Sacred, the relationship becomes a contemplative one. A relationship may be as brief as a thirty-second conversation or as long as a lifetime. Most fall somewhere in between. We choose both consciously and unconsciously with whom to connect and, in doing so, create a dynamic, intricate, ever-evolving constellation.

Being in contemplative relationship requires that we experience life outside the comfortable parameters of unaware relationship. When we are unaware, we may find our self in a tumultuous relationship with another simply because it is easier to stay than to leave. We do not understand the potential that exists by disengaging from the relationship. I didn't leave my relationship immediately. Although we attempted to repair the cracks, it became apparent almost two years after my move that this connection needed to shift into a different kind of relationship.

Each time a relationship shifts, we have the chance to see the other's divine spark and respond with unconditional love and compassion. Living in awareness opens our eyes to opportunities that exist to create poignant interactions and to then reverence those changes. Each connection leaves indelible marks on our essence. With awareness, we grasp onto opportunities presented through a change in relationship status. Living within the intricate connections of our constellation leads us to a place of personal and relational transformation.

Connections created through awareness are contemplative ones. These connections occur with our self, others, all creation, and with the Sacred itself. In contemplative relationships we see the Sacred in each partner. We may more easily recognize the extraordinary in our relationships with family members, loved ones, and friends. Often we fail to recognize or identify our other relationships. We may not identify our connections with coworkers, colleagues, neighbors, acquaintances, and strangers as actual relationships.

We have literally thousands of connections and interactions throughout the day. Each glance, smile, or gesture creates an intangible connection through which relationship is forged. A kind word or a hurtful gesture directed toward a stranger impacts another far longer than we may realize. When we are aware of our capacity to impact the life of another, our worldview and our understanding of our responsibilities to others shift. We recognize the privilege and opportunity to connect within each interaction.

It is easy to ignore a person who is homeless or someone who is trying to merge into traffic. We are not invested in that person and may never see him or her again. We don't live with a constant reminder of those interactions. Yet these spontaneous connections with an unknown person contain the seeds of radical transformation. Any kindness has the potential to grow exponentially, as does any careless act. All interactions have unknown, long-term consequences. In each of our interactions, we have the opportunity to make a difference and to have a difference made to us.

A kind word, opening a door, allowing someone to merge into traffic may quiet anxiety, put a smile on another's face, and enable that person to pay the action forward. As that kindness and that compassion travel across the connection, they don't stop. They glide across the connections of one constellation to the constellation of another. Who knows where the essence of our compassion shows up?

important to remember

dominos

The same is true of our connections with all aspects of creation. Responding to an animal, petting or playing with a pet, picking up litter, appreciating nature as we walk impact us. The parts of creation that are human-formed are important as well. How we connect with cars, computers, phones, bikes, coffee makers—you get the idea—reflect who we are. Reverence or deep respect is the intentional attitude to carry in all these relationships.

Our relationship with the Sacred is integral to each part of our day. This is what holds all of our relationships together. While some might name the Sacred as a specific deity and within the confines of a specific religious or spiritual tradition, others may define the Sacred differently. Within the context of this book, I ask that you define Sacred for yourself. Each of us carries specific thoughts as to what is Sacred, a definition as personal as the individual's relationship with it. For me, the Sacred lives in the extraordinary found in every moment, and each of us holds a spark of the Sacred within us.

God or the dignity + human right a person has

The relationship we have with our self is perhaps most fraught with issues and disconnects. We love our self, dislike our self, feel connected, or are disconnected. We may be unconscious of how our thoughts, words, and actions impact us. Through the many facets of our self, we create an internal constellation. With awareness and intent, we strip away our illusions and anchor to our authentic self. Perhaps we believe that we are unable to commit to losing weight. That belief may be an illusion that is hiding our true fear of life changes that will occur with weight loss. When we understand the illusion, we open our self to transformation. *← Amen!*

Our relationship with our self forms the foundation of our connections with others. Becoming aware of the impact of our words, thoughts, and actions on our self is vital to building sustainable connections with others. A healthy connection with our self ensures our ability to create and maintain healthy relationships with others, creation, and the Sacred.

Our constellation of connections has three elements: silence, compassion, and communion. Each element is vital and necessary in the creation and maintenance of thriving relationships. Unless we are living contemplatively, we may not notice one of the components is either diminished or missing.

The inky night sky in which our connections thrive is silence. Living within an environment of silence, we recognize the potential and power of intimate relationship. Silence is more than a cessation of noise. Within this space our awareness is heightened. Within the inky night sky, we gain clarity and the ability to recognize our distractions. Our distractions may be thoughts that draw us away from the present moment or a series of tasks that keep us too busy to focus on our authentic reality

In this place of silence, we can choose not to be triggered by our emotions to react. Instead, we can acknowledge our distractions and respond with compassion to our self and others. We recognize the potential fibers , the aspects of a person or our self that invite us into relationship, that could twine in connection with others. We act in ways that empower us to connect with others.

Deep serenity and peace are birthed and flow from silence. Within this space we are more receptive to forming meaningful connections. We are more aware of each moment in which we live our life. Here we are more likely to be the objective observer. We notice and own our judgments, assumptions, and agendas. With this recognition comes the power of choice. We can choose to react to the distractions in hurtful or harmful ways. Or we can choose to respond in loving, gentle, compassionate ways. (Please note that a reaction is a negative way of interacting while a response is a positive means.) Our sustainable connections are formed as a result of our responses and our loving, gentle, compassionate presence.

The twinkling stars in the night sky are all of us—divine sparks. Each twinkling star that is another invites us to potential relationship. Those sparks, our very beings, are fueled by compassion. It connects us to others through our desire to cause no harm and alleviate suffering. Compassion invites us to discover a connection that is interdependent, not codependent. Within this constellation of connections, we realize that relationships are not possible without compassion.

The final element in our night sky is the deepest form of communication, communion. Communication occurs first with our self and then expands into our relationship with the Sacred, others, and all of creation. By entering into communion we create the invisible connectors, the fibrous strands between the sparks of all creation. Moving beyond but including a verbal conversation, we enter into a place of full-body listening. Our whole body and all of our senses are engaged.

If one of these components were missing, we would be unable to create a sustainable constellation of connections. When we have not created an environment of silence, picking up minor difficulties in the relationship is difficult. For example, we may not notice that the other does not feel valued. If they try to communicate how they feel, we may react in ways that are not compassionate. Our interactions may become more superficial. We neglect to enter the deep communication that occurs when we listen and respond with our entire being.

Through contemplative relationships, we cultivate our authentic being. We no longer feel the need to cling to our illusions and inaccurate perceptions about our self. We may believe that we are not good enough or do not have the necessary skills. As we let them go, we reframe our reality into a more accurate, more authentic representation of who we are and how we interact with the world. Silence wraps us in its honest, peace-filled embrace while providing the space for us to enter into authentic, intimate relationships. Silence creates the space in which we honestly and courageously engage in self-examination. Our divine spark shines brightly with compassion, and we reach out to others in our world. When we reach out to others without agendas, we connect with full-body listening and enter into communion.

Our constellation of connections requires deep awareness and anchoring in the moment. When we are backward-focused on past regrets or forward-focused on future worries, we miss opportunities to engage the other in meaningful, heartfelt ways. Only in the moment are we fully awake and aware of potential connections and the joy that comes from these connections. No longer is our constellation of connections something that occurs out there. Each interaction becomes a vibrant extension of who we are.

No longer are we a lone star that twinkles disconnected from the rest of the vibrant night sky. We become a part of a community of beings that illuminate not only our soul essence but also the essences of all others and of all creation. We become a constellation of connections within a greater, never-ending, constantly shifting, forever-evolving constellation of connections of the global community.

Creating a Constellation of Connections

Sit quietly. Focus on your breathing. Do not try to shift your breathing by deepening it. Allow it to naturally flow in and out. Reflect upon your key relationships. Name those that seem most important.

On a sheet of paper, begin to create your constellation of connections. First, place yourself on the sheet as the North Star. Then begin to place on the sheet other stars that represent your key relationships.

Connect the stars to you. If they are connected to one another, draw those lines as well.

You may choose to return to this sheet several times in the upcoming days to add additional stars/compassion sparks.

Chapter 2

Connecting Contemplatively

Contemplative relationships require full engagement in each interaction. If we are not intentional, we flit from one relationship to another. This brilliant world of connections may be brittle and superficial. Instead of flitting, we choose to look for ways to strengthen each connection through each interaction. When we engage another contemplatively, even the briefest interaction has the opportunity to change the landscape of our being. Relationships offer glimpses into who we are authentically. These catalysts hold the potential to transform our very existence.

Words mean different things to different people and in different situations. The word "contemplative" is one such word, and the meaning of the word "contemplative relationship" may be confusing. I once heard a guest on a news show talking about contemplating war, as in considering the possibility of war. His use of the word did not hold the same meaning as mine does in writing about contemplative relationships.

Although a word's definition is found in the dictionary, it also has cultural, communal, and contextual meanings. An individual may also use inflections, gestures, and other body language that cast a different meaning on what is said. The word contemplative is both difficult to pronounce and to define.

Being contemplative, for me, is focusing my awareness on the Sacred in the present moment. Through this awareness, I experience the extraordinary strands of others and all of creation that connect me to my life-weave and the greater weave of all. In these moments of being present, I have the power of choice: Will I react in harmful or hurtful ways, or will I respond with unconditional love and compassion? In each moment that I act with compassion for my self and others, I connect contemplatively with my self, the Sacred, others, and all of creation.

We have the power and ability to create and sustain contemplative relationships. A contemplative relationship is one in which we live in deep awareness while connecting to the extraordinary or what we hold in deep reverence in another. In our awareness, the possibility of these connections becomes visible. We may notice that a friend may need us to listen and provide support, or we may choose to allow a stranger to merge into traffic in front of us. With each of these opportunities taken, we are able to connect contemplatively in that moment and every aspect of our life. When we shift our way of being in relationship, the way we experience life shifts and our worldview transforms.

No longer does what divides us seem important. Instead, we dissolve barriers, celebrate differences, and endeavor to find common ground. Contemplative relationships invite us to enter into a new paradigm, leading us to the awareness that we live in a world fraught with an old, static way of being. The new paradigm is filled with uncertainties while the old way is known. It is often easier to stay in the old instead of trying something new. The transition to this way of life is not easy, but it is filled with deeper, more joy-filled, intimate connections.

How we react or respond within our interactions determines if we are creating a contemplative way of life or operating from old paradigms and living as is instead of living all that could be. When we choose to react out of fear, we cause harm and damage to the connections we have created. Responding with unconditional love and compassion is the catalyst that releases our authentic essence from the well of our being. When we respond this way, we recognize the traps laid by our triggers and circumvent them. Another person may do or say something that causes us to react in anger. The anger may have little to do with the other person and everything with how we perceive our self. We may view our self as not being competent in some arena and the words or actions of another may emphasize this illusion. The trap laid by our trigger is our reaction to the other. When we recognize this trap, we gain a greater awareness of the catalysts that bring those feelings to the surface.

It is not enough to recognize these triggers. Through reflection, introspection, and integration of what we discover, we can identify but not be swayed by our distractions. We choose not to allow our triggers to distract us; rather, we interact in ways that show our authentic nature. Each compassionate response aligns us with our contemplative rhythm. We intuitively focus our awareness in the present moment. Our need to react to grievances diminishes; our desire to respond authentically becomes our motivation.

Living contemplatively invites us to experience all of life through full-body listening and compassionate response. Our mental, physical, emotional, and spiritual bodies align to create a poignancy of awareness. The world may seem brighter, and our senses more refined. We sense the extraordinary and the possible. All five of our senses move in harmony. We hear the words, see what is being said, notice body language, pick up clues through our senses of smell and taste. Our entire being is aware of our impact on others. When we truly engage in full-body listening and compassionate response, we leave no room to be anywhere but in the present moment.

With this awareness comes responsibility. No longer can we go through life ignorant and unconscious of how we affect the world. We listen to our internal monologue and recognize the roots of our thoughts—our judgments, assumptions, and beliefs. The roots of our thoughts burst through the ground of our being and unfold as the flowers of our words and actions. We are mindful of the garden we create as we acknowledge the impact of our thoughts, words, and actions. A practicing contemplative makes choices with a commitment to respond to life from this place of awareness. The intent is to minimize the harm caused by our words, thoughts, and actions and to take advantage of opportunities to respond with compassion.

A contemplative life is seldom experienced in a vacuum or as a solitary being. A contemplative life occurs in relationship. Our contemplative spirit is reflected in each of our relationships: be that with our self, the Sacred, others, or any aspect of creation. Not a moment of our life goes by without connecting. In our constellation, living with awareness means we choose to live in intimate relationship instead of skimming the surface of connection.

We choose how we experience life: Do we open our eyes with curious daring and see the extraordinary or do we trudge though life only seeing the mundane and lackluster? Building a contemplative relationship means we have chosen to respond with curious daring and embrace the extraordinary. No longer do we willingly rest in the mundane world.

The root of each relationship lies in the ground of our being. For us to successfully connect with another, our relationship with our self must be authentic, humble, and honest. Our words and actions provide clues to the health and integrity of a relationship. We may react to triggers and create illusions that weaken the connection to our truth. These fear-filled illusions create a shaky foundation upon which other relationships rest.

If we react with anger, we may identify as an angry person. Or, if we feel insecure, we may judge our self as needy. Both of these are illusions created by imbalances in our relationship with self. Unless we recognize what is triggering these reactions, we are unable to strengthen and repair the foundation for our other relationships.

Humility empowers us to look intentionally at all our actions. When we are humble, we acknowledge the illusions while celebrating the parts of us that are authentic and honest. By releasing our illusions and holding firmly to what is real and true, our relationship with our self thrives. As we thrive, the brokenness in our foundation heals. The cracks in the foundation mend and the light of our inner core reaches out to others in connection.

Only in those moments of connection do we begin to dig deeply into the ground of our being. Here we understand who we are and identify the paradox—the ways our illusions obscure what is our truth— in which we live. We never stop searching for and releasing illusions while acknowledging that we need humility.

Rather than debasing our self, we recognize what needs to shift and identify what is our truth. Silently and without fanfare, we take steps to transformation.

Our perception of the world and how we relate to it, both individually and as a whole, are grounded in our relationship with our self. We can form thriving relationships only through an ongoing query of our thoughts, words, and actions in light of our authentic nature. This examination clears the path to better understanding how we form our beliefs, make judgments, and draw assumptions. We gain our truth by challenging our perceptions. Only then do we develop and deepen the relationship with our self. This identification, releasing our illusions, and embracing our authentic nature create the anchor point from which all of our relationships stem.

The relationship with our self is the core connection in our constellation. Without a strong, authentic relationship with self, our other relationships would be shaky and illusion-based. Understanding who we are not only provides the base on which we live authentically and honestly but also creates the structure on which our authentic and honest relationships thrive. Our other contemplative relationships provide the nourishment for us to strengthen the relationship with self. For example, through our connection to the Sacred we gain clarity about who we are. With this self-understanding, we recognize how the Sacred manifests in our life. We recognize that the Sacred is present in each of our other relationships.

As we deepen our relationship with the Sacred, we redefine or fine-tune who we are and the role that the Divine holds in our life. Thomas Merton reminds us that "the spiritual life is first of all a life."[1] Everything we do is in relationship with the Sacred and a reflection of that relationship. In every moment of our life, whether we are aware or not, we are in conversation with the Divine.

For me that conversation, while including traditional prayer, also incorporates all our thoughts, words, and actions. At the end of the day, I reflect upon how my life mirrored my spiritual being. At times what I think, say, and do is not the prayer I had hoped to form throughout the day. Simultaneously aware of our internal and external conversations, we better understand how our judgments, assumptions, and beliefs are formed and sustained. Only on this path of understanding do we gain the courage to question and challenge our beliefs and judgments. Through this compassionate challenging, we strengthen not only our relationship with our self but also our relationship with the Sacred and ultimately with each of our relationships.

Our relationship with the Sacred is multifaceted and unending. The Sacred for each of us is personal and is mirrored in our thoughts, words, and actions. When we rest in the silence of our quiet mind, we hear through full-body listening the response of the Sacred to our questions and comments. Benedict of Nursia in The Rule encouraged us to "listen…with the ear of your heart."[2] Listening with the ear of our heart requires an engagement of all of our senses. Through this engagement, our connection to the Spirit becomes a conduit for gathering information. Through intentional listening, we gain clues to living more deeply and intimately.

Each relationship in which we engage has two anchor points. The first is our self; the second is the Sacred. When we connect in relationship with another or any aspect of creation, we form a relationship triad. Full-body listening strengthens the anchor points and energizes the connections. When we listen with our entire being, our five primary senses are engaged. We notice how our physical body is impacted. Our relationship with the Sacred underlies and empowers us to act with unconditional love and compassion.

Being with others can rocket us to the heights of joy or plummet us into the depths of despair. Most often we find our self in the middle ground. In this place we may exist in a relationship while not entering deeply into the connection. We can remain in this middle place or we can choose to release our autopilot and enter deeply into our contemplative stance. In this place we are aware of the highs, lows, and middle ground in each relationship and are able to navigate them for the benefit of all in relationship.

It is easier to see the impact we have upon our family and close friends. These relationships have been developed over years.

They have comforting rhythms. We know how to nudge the other into a reaction or soothe them into a response. Often we interact on autopilot because of the level of comfort. But we can choose through our intention to connect with them in deeper, potentially more intimate ways.

Relationships with acquaintances, colleagues, and coworkers manifest differently. We maintain a level of emotional and mental distance with them and often strive to be socially and politically correct. We maintain a mask of illusion during these interactions. Instead of being honest about what we think or how we feel, we share only what we believe will be accepted.

It might seem easier not to allow others to see our authentic self. But within these connections we must ask our self if the depth of our intimacy is appropriate or if we are just engaging superficially. Creating contemplative relationships requires courage. We must be willing to listen to another and respond with genuine compassion. This may mean moving past what is socially acceptable and meeting another where they are. Moving past the superficial, we get to know another and serve as companions on the learning journey.

Another relationship is that with the stranger. We often deny or ignore these connections. It can be difficult to understand why we would want to connect with a random person. When we explore our inability to connect, we expose those facets where growth is not only possible but needed. Having a conversation with a stranger in line at a coffee shop often provides opportunities for growth.

We ignore not only the stranger. At times we are not present to a loved one or are too busy pushing our own agenda. If we consciously change the subject when a friend is trying to express feelings or judging the actions of another, we are not interacting from our authentic core. We are operating from the illusion that ignoring what is uncomfortable lessens its impact on our authentic reality. When we acknowledge the other with the intent to understand, we move past the discomfort of interacting. By acknowledging the other, we respond with compassion and, in doing so, create a contemplative relationship.

Accepting opportunities to interact with a stranger invites us into deep, intimate connection and a greater understanding of both our light and shadow sides. Often we are the beneficiaries of great intangible gifts when we spontaneously connect. We may discover a friend for life, alter our perceptions, or radically change our worldview. When we enter into a relationship with curious daring, the outcome may be surprising and life-altering.

Our relationship with creation is the last of the four core relationships. We ask the same questions that we ask in all relationships:

- How do I interact with non-human sentient beings?
- What is my relationship with the natural world?
- How do I treat inanimate objects?

The answers to these questions are couched in this suggestion from the Rule of St. Benedict: "Treat all as vessels of the altar."[3] For me, this is a reminder that every person, every living being, everything in creation is a mirror of the Sacred, a sacred vessel. Therefore, we should treat every person, every sentient being, everything with reverence and compassion. I, too, am a sacred vessel, a mirror of the Sacred. I see the Sacred in all; the extraordinary is reflected in me. I act in ways accentuating my sacred nature. In this way I brighten the lights of the Sacred Constellation.

Relationships encourage me to really look at my life. When I am honest, relationship allows me to uncover the illusions within me. With humility, I am able to release the illusions and bask in the light of my authentic self. No longer am I alone for I see how my thoughts, words, and actions impact the greater world.

Relationship permeates every aspect and facet of our life. When we live in awareness of the potential for relationship, our perception of reality shifts. We may gain greater clarity of our life purpose. Life is no longer us against them or treating something as less. Rather, we look to connect in meaningful, loving ways in our four core relationships: with our self, the Sacred, others, and all of creation. These connections are often the impetus to shift the way we perceive the world. They challenge our beliefs and judgments.

We are no longer in a static relationship; we are with another creating a connection of equal partners. Living in contemplative relationship, we discover what Thomas Merton calls an "older unity where we are all one."[4] Any illusion of separateness evaporates, and we clearly live within the connections that create our constellation.

Creating a Constellation of Connections

Sit quietly. Focus on your breathing. Do not try to shift your breathing. Allow it to naturally flow in and out. Don't deepen your inhale/exhale. Just notice.

Reflect upon your relationship with self. Create a constellation of connections that focuses solely on aspects of self. These aspects may be personality traits, roles that you assume, emotions, thought patterns, or those parts of you that you view as relevant. Name your being—those that are authentic and those that cast illusion. It is important to identify both the true self as well as any masks. Create this microcosm of connection.

(Keep both your created constellation from the previous chapter and this one together.)

Chapter 3

Our Divine Spark, The Hub of Our Connections

Life is an intricately woven sky of connections. We reach out to one person and discover a connection with another. But, no matter where our weave twines, our constellation could not exist without the relationship to self. Our self is the hub of our interactions. It is powered by the energy of compassion that emanates from our divine spark. This part of our essence connects to the Sacred. Following the relationship pathway through our divine spark, we enter into relationship with the Sacred through the silence in our quiet mind.

The midnight sky in our constellation of connections represents the deep serenity and peace of the silence in which our quiet mind flourishes. Although silence is physically a cessation of noise, it is also the environment in which we enter into hyperawareness. Within this space we objectively notice and identify our distractions. We name what is authentic, acknowledge and release illusions, and reframe our life situation. We gain clarity.

Within silence exists the space for us to honestly connect. Here we courageously engage in self-examination. We intentionally seek to connect with our divine spark. Through this connection we discover the limitless possibility of relationship. We live with the potential for unity with all of creation.

Jewish mysticism speaks of the divine spark that is present at the center of all beings. We are gifted with this glowing ember at the conception of our spirit. It is the part of the Sacred we carry with us from the beginning into the forever. Our divine spark connects us to all of creation. Each moment that we enter into relationship intentionally or unconsciously, our divine spark flares across the connection to the other. Our sparking energies weave together. With this twining of flames, our connection deepens and the light of the Sacred burns brighter across the connection and within each of us.

Divine light warmly fills us and is a beacon that guides us to authentic living. We begin the journey of tikkun hanefesh, or the healing of our self. This healing creates a solid, authentic foundation within us. Upon this foundation, we create all other relationships. As we acknowledge the illusions that prevent us from deeply loving our self and as we practice self-compassion, we discover the joy that lies within our authentic being.

When we live authentically, the light of our spark draws us to others and draws others to us. The divine spark is fueled by all forms of compassion—for our self, shared with others, received from the Sacred and from others. Our interactions fuel the twinkling light of our spark. These connections empower us to engage in tikkun olam, or the repair of the world. Within our relationships, we join with others in the repair work. Tikkun hanefesh and tikkun olam cannot exist independently of one another. Each is an important tool to use in all core relationships.[5]

Compassion is an integral part of all creation. It permeates every aspect and facet of our life, even if we are unable to sense it. It emanates from each of our divine sparks. We draw upon the essence of compassion shared in each moment that we alleviate suffering. Compassion mingles with our intent and flows deeply into our self, healing old hurts and suffering. With this compassion, we reach out to others.

Our divine spark is also fueled by the compassionate acts of others. When another responds to us with compassion, the well of our compassion fills. Giving and receiving compassion deepens our connections. The sparks flicker through the connections, shining ever more brightly against the inky darkness of silence.

Without the intuitive sharing of compassion, we would rest in the silence of the night sky as solitaries. The twinkling stars would be islands separated by a vast inkiness. Each time we share compassion, our divine sparks connect. Communication moves across these strands and compassion flows through these twining fibers. We connect to each other through full-body listening and compassionate response.

This dialogue is a holistic form of communication called communion. Moving beyond words, we delve into this interaction with all of our senses. We engage in full-body listening by using all of our senses. Body language and pauses in conversation provide clues. This communication is with our entire being—our physical body, our emotions, our intellect, and our spirit.

Through communion, we recognize how best to interact with our entire being. We are aware of our body, mind, emotions, and spirit during any interactions. We notice and identify how another's words and actions trigger us. When we are in communion, we are fully awake and fully alive as we respond to others; we create a constellation of intentional connections.

The constellation of connections mirrors the ebb and flow of our relationships. Relationships are seldom static; they are fluid and dynamic. Through the silence in our quiet mind, we achieve awareness that helps us maintain these connections. We are aware of potential and actual shifts in relationships. We notice when someone's actions are out of the norm. Perhaps they are more distant and unapproachable. Or they may seem to need more support. By identifying this shift in our partner's behavior, we can craft appropriate responses.

Relationship cannot thrive unless we are flexible and dynamic in our responses. This may mean putting aside our judgment, assumptions, and fears as we compassionately explore what lies at the root of the other's behavior. With this stance, we understand that another's actions may not be reflective of our interactions. Relationships do not exist in vacuums. We may react to another not based upon what they said but upon what we believe they mean. Through full-body listening we better understand how we are triggered and how to circumvent reactions. Our reactions serve as catalysts to help us identify our illusions and our authenticity.

Each relationship has the capacity to teach us much about our self. Our divine spark hub would slumber in isolation were we not aware of our relationships with others and with creation. Fellow sojourners provide opportunities to meet life challenges though we may refuse to accept the lessons. Relationship requires courageous response in order to actualize our life purpose.

Our constellation's configuration constantly shifts. If we are not alert to the person or nuances in a situation, we disconnect or become estranged. At other times, we are fully present in and aware of the relationship while it shifts. We notice that the connection is weakening and may choose to gently allow the relationship to shift. A relationship may end no matter what we do. We can choose to respond to ending a relationship in ways that are gentle or we can react by ending a relationship in hurtful ways.

Relationships are fluid. Some deepen while others end. When a connection is broken, we can honor the time spent in relationship and rejoice in the lessons learned and the loved shared. Relationships create the space for loving and celebrating and learning to flourish. Through these connections we share compassion. Within each connection lies the possibility for our divine spark to connect with another.

Our intentions manifest in our actions. Through our actions, we fuel the divine spark of another. Communion is the avenue through which we feed the divine spark of another. When we are in sync through communion, we recognize when to strengthen the connection and when to move into another phase of the relationship.

Our constellation of connections is organic and flexible only when our hub flares with self-compassion. An authentic relationship with our self creates the core from which other relationships grow. When we are mindful, we can make the choice to live authentically. Our authentic presence impacts our relationships with others and configures our contemplative constellation of connections.

We do not know the impact of a thirty-second conversation or a thirty-year friendship. Every person and every thing we come into contact with are represented within our constellation. All are meaningful. All impact our divine spark. While we may not immediately understand their importance, in time we may understand how those relationships altered our relationship with self. If the actions of another triggered anger in use, we may believe that we are an angry person. Later, we may discover that the anger was the reaction and that at its roots were fears of loss. Only in the present can we name our roots and negate the illusions our relationships created and respond in loving, gentle, compassionate ways.

Creating an authentic, contemplative constellation of connections requires integrity, honesty, and courage. Without these core strengths, the hub of our divine spark is weakened. Perhaps we lack the courage to initiate a connection or we may, without integrity, enter into a relationship for selfish, agenda-driven reasons. With honesty we question our role in the relationship and listen to the answers. Courage impels us to fully engage others in ways that build meaningful connections. We seek the best course for creating and sustaining an authentic contemplative relationship.

Integrity, honesty, and courage are conceived and grown in the silence of our quiet mind. In this environment we reflect upon the relationship. This reflection incorporates an awareness of our feelings, judgments, and beliefs about this relationship. We actively search for any distractions that prevent us from being authentic. We are aware without attaching to a particular outcome, not judging, being violent, or defending our position. We identify our triggers and admit how we react. We integrate our understanding from reflection and introspection into our relationships. This integration paves the way for more contemplative relationships.

Through the awareness gained during reflection, we reveal the multilayers of the relationship. These layers include how our connection with the other nourishes our constellation as a whole.

Through the knowledge gained, we gain clues to strengthen other relationships. Each relationship connects us to our self and to the greater community. The more intentional we are in relationship, the more layers are revealed.

Awareness and reflection empower us on the path of conscious relationship. We have the power to choose to intentionally embrace opportunities for intimacy. This intimacy is about sharing a part of our self—body, mind, spirit, or heart. It can occur in an instant or occur over time. Through intimacy, we develop an environment conducive to individual and relational growth. We are aware of how choosing to respond affects the other and the connection between us. We strive to minimize our negative reactions and blind choices. When we are fully aware, we have the power to make choices couched in compassion.

Full-body listening and compassionate response are tools used to discern our role in the relationship and the role of the relationship in our life. Full-body listening requires attending to the five primary senses as we are aware of our reactions and the reactions of others. We direct both full-body listening and compassionate response toward our internal monologue and to our many external dialogues. With all of our senses we discern if the relationship, in its current form, is life-giving.

When we meet someone, we may ask how they are without expecting an answer. Instead of saying hello, this may be our greeting. This way of interacting creates a static relationship. Non-contemplative relationships are static; we may feel we are following a script. Our flexible, dynamic, evolving relationships are contemplative.

Through intentional interactions our relationships evolve. Instead of asking "How are you doing?" as a greeting, we are prepared to listen to how the other truly is. This way of connecting requires that we are fully aware and present while being committed to transformation. Growth in relationship requires constant awareness, honesty, and courage. The benefits reaped while in this stance are exponential.

Preparing to listen to a response does not mean we develop a long-term relationship. It means that we are connecting in ways that acknowledge the other in the moment of connection. In the same way, long-term relationships may grow for specific purposes. A relationship with a therapist may be filled with trust but never become close. The same may be true of coworkers. A contemplative relationship is built upon an awareness of the reasons for connection. We attend to those reasons with a dynamic, flexible stance.

We grow and evolve as our relationships grow and evolve. What once began as a business association may morph into friendship. A close friendship may shift to an acquaintanceship. In the same respect, a chance encounter with a stranger may shift over time into a lifelong friendship. Our role is to be aware of the nuances in the relationship and be open to transformation instead of second-guessing or making selfish choices. At times I have wanted to build a friendship with another because I admired them. But, over time, I discovered that the little we had in common meant that the foundation of friendship was impossible to sustain.

While the nature of your interactions may change from a close friendship to an acquaintanceship, it may be no less life-giving for you and the other person. My son and I moved at the end of his fourth-grade year. I made several friendships with the parents of his new friends. At the end of the year, both students went on to different middle schools. I eventually lost contact with one parent; the other I now see irregularly.

Relationships may become more life-giving after a transition. After I left a job, I had opportunities to turn what had been a colleague relationship into a friendship. Engaging in contemplative relationships requires accepting any changes as opportunities to be fully present and responsive to the world around us. With this stance we are able to be present in unconditional, compassionate ways.

There are no rules regarding the dynamics of relationship. We must be open to what we and the other need in the relationship. For this, we trust our internal monitor. By navigating through the silence of our quiet mind with compassion and a willingness to communicate deeply, we expand our realm of possibilities revealed through inner wisdom.

Communicating deeply means no longer believing, without input from the other, that we understand their point of view. When we listen and dialogue with our self and others, we attend to our judgments and assumptions. Instead of reacting out of them, we respond to knowledge gained. Our world expands in phenomenal ways. We learn to be present to others in ways that are expansive to both parties. We live in a deeper unity and deeper connectivity. This paradigm shift is possible when responding compassionately from our quiet mind.

Although there are no set rules for building and sustaining relationships, this does not mean that we toss out our set of personal values. We engage each relationship with personal integrity and awareness. This may be as simple as agreeing to cause no harm, being compassionate, and being realistic about the relationship.

While our goal is to be compassionately honest and cause no harm, interacting with another can be a scary proposition. Unless we engage in communion, we cannot be courageously honest about our fears and perceived wants and needs in the relationship. One of my needs is punctuality. Expressing this need could potentially open the relationship to discord. My intent is to express this need in ways that are gentle and gracious.

Each moment of connection is an opportunity to embrace our inner courageous being and strengthen our inner hub, our divine spark. We strive for clarity to understand our self and others. This includes being clear about our needs and desires and how they align with the needs and desires of the other. When we are honest about our needs and desires, our integrity deepens.

Through this integrity, we clearly articulate our needs and desires, and we sincerely want to understand the needs and desires of another. It is only through integrity that we gain clarity to create, navigate, and deepen our connections. We share the understanding gained in ways that benefit and strengthen our connection with the other and all of the connections within our constellation.

Creating a Constellation of Connections

The midnight sky represents the deep serenity and peace of the silence of our quiet mind.

Sit quietly. Focus on your breathing. Do not try to shift your breathing. Allow it to naturally flow in and out. Don't shift your inhale/exhale. Just notice.

Spend some time in conversation with your divine spark. What illusions surface about recent interactions? Are you identifying with a negative certain emotion? How are you authentic? What attributes or traits do you have that bring you closer to awareness?

How are illusions preventing you from being in a contemplative relationship? (Think about a recent interaction that triggered a reaction in you.)

What parts of your authentic self encourage contemplative relationship? (Think about a recent interaction in which a reaction was circumvented and you responded instead.)

How are you aware of your feelings, judgments, and beliefs and how they create a contemplative relationship?

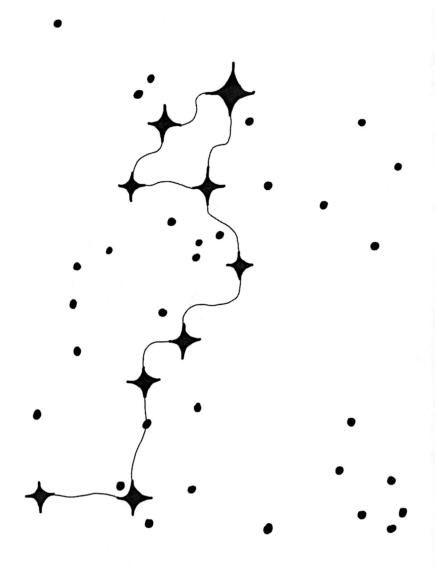

Night sky = silence.
Stars = compassion.
Lines of Connection = communion.

Chapter 4

Relationships: Engaged, Dynamic, Flexible

Contemplative relationships are engaged relationships. Often a second marriage will exhibit characteristics of a contemplative relationship that the earlier marriage didn't. The partners may be more present to one another and more intentional in how they communicate. Instead of being two individuals with separate goals, they find ways to maintain individual identities while forming a cohesive connection. This relationship is dynamic and fluid.

Contemplative relationships are the avenues through which we live dynamically and with flexibility. When we are fully engaged, we more easily notice the subtleties in a relationship. We realize that sure pathways of growth lie in relationships. Any discomforts or irritation help us transform into our true, authentic self. Pema Chödrön reminds us that "the more we relate with others, the more quickly we discover where we're blocked."[6] This realization nudges us along the path of personal evolution.

As we evolve, we strengthen our connections and serve as a catalyst for the evolution of another's authentic self. To increase authenticity in a relationship requires that we interact with honesty and courage while being open and creative in our responses. Within this way of interacting, contemplative relationships emerge. We are free to explore without judging or defending the depth of connection we find in each moment of every day. If a relationship seems superficial, it may be exactly what we need to be in authentic connection with the other. Our role is to be in the relationship as a partner not as a director.

When we live in awareness and consciously seek to understand the other, we form community through relationship. This community becomes ever more diverse as we enter into a collective where we understand and respect the other even when we do not agree. Within this stance lies the extraordinarily transformative power of contemplative relationship.

Our commitment to being respectful and to seeking understanding is important to the health and balance of any relationship. Respect is vital. With respect we honestly access understanding. We question what confuses us. Respect, honesty, and understanding are key to maintaining a vital, strong connection with another.

Using reflection and introspection, we discern the common ground of a relationship. More than what partners have in common, this is a place of deep commitment and respect. In this common ground, the relationship has the best chance of evolving. None of us remains unchanged throughout our life. Living requires that we grow physically, emotionally, mentally, and spiritually. In order for us to continue in any relationship, both partners must change. This does not mean the relationship always continues. Contemplatively, a relationship may end while providing each partner with insights and opportunities for growth.

In my practice as an Intuitive, I work with individuals who want to create durable relationships. As they learn and grow, I am offered opportunities to grow as well. After my client reaches a certain stage of growth, our relationship often ends. Both of us are prepared to enter into new relationships.

Discernment is a conscious, intentional way of reflection and introspection. It requires a full-body, multi-sensory search to understand what is occurring. Perhaps we have a niggling feeling that a relationship has veered off course or no longer brings us to a place of peace-filled balance. Using all our senses, we become more aware of what is triggering these feelings. This initial full-body assessment provides insights that may include perceived failures.

Self-compassion allows us to move past any perceived self-failures; compassion directed toward others provides a balm to get past any sore spots in that relationship. We have to be courageous and willing to take a long, loving look at the current situation with open eyes. Only then are we able to decide how to respond to the other.

This long, loving look begins when we focus, through our senses, on our reaction and response to another or a given situation. Moving beyond the sensations, we begin to explore what lies at the root. For example, I had a very good friend who embraced God as a woman. Each time I would refer to God as a man, she would loudly correct me. Upon reflection and introspection, I reclaimed my belief that God was neither male nor female. I also admitted that I felt belittled and bullied by her comments. I discovered these important roots of my reactions by using the 4nons.

The 4nons—nonattachment, nonjudgment, nondefensiveness, and nonviolence—are important tools not only in the discernment process but also in all aspects of relationship. The 4nons are not negative; rather, each invites us into the stance of the objective observer. We notice what is occurring while not reacting in harsh, critical ways.

Whatever we discover during reflection and introspection, we agree to accept without attachment. We hold our knowledge and understanding lightly, not twisting it to suit us in attempting to deepen a relationship with someone who is an acquaintance. Instead of forcing a friendship, I remind myself that creating a deeper connection might actually destroy our fragile bond. My best course is to allow it to grow and deepen naturally. This is an aspect of being dynamic and flexible.

Instead of labeling or judging what happens, I take cues from the other. This is not always easy. In a dating relationship, one person may be farther along the romance pathway and falsely judge or label an action of another as lack of interest or fear. Another may judge their partner as too clingy and overinvolved.

When we engage the 4nons, we willingly step outside what we think we want and live differently; we try something new. We don't defend either our perceptions or our actions. As an objective observer we are cautious about deepening or ending a relationship. We use full-body listening to perceive the cues and then respond in loving, gentle ways. The first 3nons pave the way for our nonviolent heart. When incorporating the 4nons into our interactions, we learn the lessons inherent in the relationship.

The 4nons are part of relationship discernment. Discernment happens in our place of silence. Within the silence, we filter the distractions and gain clarity. This clarity invites us to explore, through reflections, attributes that strengthen relationships and those that weaken our connections. We then use introspection to examine the roots of issues and discover possible resolutions. Discernment requires that we integrate what we have discovered during reflections and introspection.

Once silence is created, we wake up our quiet mind. With our quiet mind we recognize opportunities to move past reactions that are triggered by distractions. Within our quiet mind we are aware of how we cling too tightly, act upon our judgments, hide behind our fears by defending, and subtly and overtly act in violent ways. We form plans of action and initiate them.

The RI^2 process—reflection, introspection, and integration—is beneficial to the discernment process. RI^2 is a holistic practice that requires the stance of objective observer. This is an attitude of a wise listener who notices but does not act upon emotions, thoughts, and actions. RI^2 has three phases: reflection, introspection, and integration. The first, reflection, requires mindful gathering of information through full-body listening. Introspection, the second phase, brings us into our mind. Here we search for patterns, gain understanding, and begin the reframing process. With integration, the final step, we try new ways of being that move us into transformation.

Before reading this section, choose a situation that concerns you. Then use the following process to gain clarity and understanding.

Reflection: Sit quietly as you become aware of your emotions, beliefs, judgments, thoughts, and physical reactions to internal and external triggers. (An internal trigger may be something you hear in your internal monologue like, "you are stupid." An external trigger may be someone who holds the door open for everyone but you.) As much as possible, remain in the stance of objective observer. Do not attach to an emotion or thought; instead, acknowledge them and gently let them go. When you become aware of a judgment, take care not to react from it. Identify any violent thoughts, but do not cling to them or react out of them. Finally, during reflection, do not defend your position. (Reflection is a means to explore your emotions, thoughts, and physical reactions while gathering information.)

Introspection: Strive to better understand your reactions and responses. Explore your behavior patterns. Remember, although two people may say the same thing, only one may trigger a reaction. During introspection, seek to understand why you react in harmful, hurtful ways and why you respond unconditionally and with compassion. Then look for ways to shift your reactions into responses. (Introspection uses our analytical and logical mind. During both reflection and introspection we never stop being an objective observer who is looking for ways to shift behavior.)

Engaging in reflection and introspection may be uncomfortable and scary. We may expose parts of our self that are not pleasant and may even be embarrassing. Who wants to don the energetic shroud of embarrassment? I often tell my program participants that when I get embarrassed, I am more likely to change. Great opportunities exist within our discomfort. We do not have to share this information with anyone. It is enough that we acknowledge our shadow. Owning this part of our self requires that we deepen the connection to the Sacred. RI^2 offers us a different way, a new path that leads to radical change within our self. And that pathway is integration.

Finally, we integrate what we have learned into our actions. This step is one of trial and error. We may have to return to the first two steps of RI^2 if we need to discover creative ways of compassionately connecting with another. The goal is not to perfectly and seamlessly transform our behavior. Rather, we continue to fine-tune our interactions so that it becomes easier to respond instead of react. We have this lifetime to explore and refine our responses and choose not to act on our distractions in reactive ways.

Through RI^2, we develop a new understanding of relationship and create ways of interacting and communicating that deepen the intimacy of our relationships. Through reflection, we listen with the ear of our heart and discover our feelings about the relationship, our partner, and our role in this connection. During introspection, we use our logical mind to identify what engages us and what is causing consternation. With integration, we use the knowledge gained in reflection and the understanding obtained in introspection to make potentially life-altering changes. This process occurs in our quiet mind.

Contemplative practice creates the environment of silence in our quiet mind. In the place of silence, we distinguish both the overt and subtle ways that we interact while acknowledging what is beneficial to the relationship and what causes harm or hurt. Through discernment, we gain clarity of the connection between the root cause of our actions and the effects they have upon our self and others.

Recognizing that reactions do not occur in a vacuum opens us to the realization that blaming is a simplistic and false way of explaining a reaction. Thinking that others are at fault for our reaction creates an illusory space. Triggers and our reactions to them are multidimensional. With this acknowledgement comes a greater understanding and acceptance of our role in triggering a fear-filled reaction or a compassionate response. As we accept responsibility for our role in the relationship, the connection shifts from subsistence to being wonderfully complex, alive, and fruitful.

With discernment we come to a profound and sometimes difficult realization about whether the relationship is supportive or toxic. Using the RI^2 process enables us to name without judgment how the relationship is not good for us. If the relationship has toxic components, we can seek alternatives to relationship-as-usual. We explore paths to release the toxins and seed a way that leads to personal and relationship transformation.

As a child grows, a parent must be able to grow with that child. Although my son lived with me during his freshman year of college, he was exploring new freedoms. I had to adapt to this shift of my son from child to young adult. I learned to be present and supportive in ways that allowed him self-discovery. Had I continued to maintain the same rules and expectations, the relationship would have been poisoned. We creatively shifted from a potentially toxic connection into a healthier, more life-giving one.

Unfortunately, some relationships do not change. For whatever reason, partners are unable to shift into a different way of relating. Some stay in those relationships because they feel they have no other alternative. Those relationships devolve into static, non-contemplative connections. For whatever reason, most of us have at least one of those relationships in our life.

Although we may be able to maintain the relationship in life-giving ways, at other times we may need to shift into a different kind of relationship. Moving from a close friendship to being acquaintances or ending a marriage is never easy, but it may be the only viable alternative for both individuals to live fully awake and fully alive.

Through discernment we courageously identify our role in the relationship. Jointly discerning with our partner is an important and necessary part of transformation. Making a unilateral decision is never the way to move forward. Only by working with the other do we formulate a response that shifts the relationship into a more life-giving and ultimately more contemplative rhythm.

Joint discernment begins much the same way as individual discernment. Both individually spend time in quiet reflection and introspection. The goal is for each partner to better understand their perceptions. Next, the partners share their realities based upon their unique perspectives. Each person usually sees the relationship differently. Next, using the 4nons, the partners share their views and decide upon the final step, integration, together.

When we cooperate and co-create, the connection becomes more intimate and secure. The static parts of the relationship are resolved, and the relationship grows into greater intimacy even if the relationship shifts in ways we grieve. Intimacy is created by authenticity, courage, and compassion. Ending a relationship with honesty and compassion is a most intimate act.

Relationship growth stems from an awareness of our thoughts, words, and actions. We accept that while they have impact in the moment, they may also have long-term consequences. We see how our actions spiral and potentially impact other aspects of our life, for all aspects of our life evolve from relationship.

In every moment we are connected in at least two relationships. Our relationships with our self and with the Sacred are never severed. Even if we are unaware of those connections, we are silently and unconsciously connected with them in the background of our life. These relationships impact all our other relationships. Developing sustainable, aware connections is vital.

We are mindful that each thought we have, word we utter, and action we take connects us to others. It does not matter if the other person is unaware of our contemplative stance toward relationship. Perhaps we are the only person who approaches the relationship in a contemplative way. Modeling contemplative behavior subtly invites others into a deeper, more intimate connection. We invite them into a peaceful way of transformation.

Over time and with patience, the contemplative nature of the relationship manifests. The other learns seemingly by osmosis as they begin to respond in ways that are intentional and filled with awareness. To a certain extent, both parties will eventually engage each other contemplatively. Do not underestimate the transformative power of your contemplative presence in relationship.

There is no science to contemplative relationship. There is no tried and true outline or course of study that will ensure that your connection with others becomes contemplative. The way of contemplative relationship invites us to blend our heart and our head in ways that make us fully present. We are asked to engage relationships with our entire being—our body, mind, spirit, and heart. Only with this holistic engagement can we be flexible as we adjust to the dynamic, changing nature of the connection.

Journeying this path requires a strong desire to compassionately connect with the other. Our way of communicating naturally shifts. We want and need to interact in ways that engage our entire body. We listen with our full body and respond compassionately.

In this deep word-filled and wordless form of communication we enter communion. Silence, compassion, and communion are the gateways through which we deepen our connections with others. Our constellation of contemplative connections is formed and strengthened through all three aspects of our night sky.

Creating a Constellation of Connections

RI² is a contemplative practice that connects our body, mind, spirit, and heart in order to respond compassionately to something in our life.

First, we reflect with our heart. We identify what we feel without making any judgment about those feelings. We observe what is happening in our life and in our relationships that might relate to what we are feeling.

Second, we introspect using our logical mind. Again, without judgment, we attempt to understand what is truly amiss.

Third, we integrate our understanding in ways that shift our fear-filled reactions to compassionate responses. More often than not, we change our thinking or behavior because we see that we were thinking and acting out of preconceptions about our self or others, rather than from knowledge and understanding.

This process, practiced regularly, transforms us. We become more true to our self and more compassionate of others.

Use the following questions to reflect, introspect, and integrate transformation into your own life. Enter into a reflective place, where you notice the many potential answers that reside in your quiet mind. Then engage your introspection. How do these responses fit with the reality of who you are? Which ones are authentic and which ones challenge your illusions? Next, integrate what you have learned by embracing what is real and true and letting go of the unreal and the untruthful. Let go of the illusion.

Sit quietly. Focus on your breathing. Do not try to shift your breathing. Allow it to naturally flow in and out. Just notice.

Using RI², reflect upon a relationship in which you and the other are in sync. Reflect upon your connection without attachment, judgment, or defensiveness. Notice what makes the relationship "easier." How does it feel to you? Describe the relationship using all of your senses.

Move into introspection. How did you reach this place of ease and wide-openness with the other? How do you communicate with the other? What patterns exist in the relationship that lend themselves to communion?

Finally, use the knowledge gained in the first two steps to shift a relationship that is not as easy. Integrate your patterns for at least seven days. Tweak if necessary.

What happens?

Chapter 5

Silence: The Inky Night Sky

In our constellation of connections silence is the inky backdrop of the night sky. Spend some time outside breathing in the darkness; engage in full-body listening by using all of your senses to discover how you are affected by your surroundings. Connect with the inky darkness of the night sky. Breathe in the dark, velvet mystery. Within this silent vastness lurk feelings and emotions that overwhelm us. In our cultivated silence lies our awareness of the roots of all our interactions and the tendrils of our distractions.

When we intentionally enter into this place of silence, we become aware of the noise in our life. We notice the many distractions that pull us from the moment and sling us into a place of reaction. Through full-body listening, we discover the obstacles that lie in the path. We may discover that the words and actions of another are triggering mistrust in us. This inability for us to trust becomes an obstacle to intimacy. By successfully maneuvering through the obstacles, we find a silent, peaceful way of being.

Silence becomes more than a mere cessation of noise. It becomes a place in which we use our entire body and all of our senses to hear clearly. We become aware of what may be preventing us from entering into relationship or encouraging intimacy with another. In the silence and through full-body listening, our divine spark connects with the spark of another.

In this awareness we notice sensory overload and take steps to minimize its impact. Overload results from an unawareness of distractions. With awareness, we gain the power of choice; we can choose to acknowledge the distractions but not be hooked by them. We remain in the moment. Present and aware, we live in conscious, contemplative relationship.

Experiencing silence connects us to the night sky in our mind. Silence is an environment that surrounds us. In the beginning the magnitude of silence may overwhelm us, triggering fear-filled reactions. When we acclimate to this place of clarity, we become calmer and enter into a hyperaware state where we intuitively know how to respond.

Our relationships with silence, others, the Sacred, and all of creation is not static. They are flexible and dynamic; They are contracting and expanding all the time. Through our responses and reactions to others, each relationship has the potential to evolve. As we practice resting in the well of unconditional love and compassion, we gain clarity of how our distractions hinder our ability to be present. In this newfound clarity we find strength to create contemplative relationships.

Deep within our essence, we unconsciously long for the physical cessation of noise, believing that this will soothe the frayed edges of our life. But we realize that silence comes in many forms—it may manifest as comforting, as awkward, and as grace-filled. Each of us has experienced these and many other visceral reactions to silence. Deepening a relationship with silence involves being comfortable with its many aspects.

While silence exists where there is no physical noise, the silence required for contemplative relationships is an environment where clarity is birthed. In this place we are asked to engage silence on multiple levels: with our physical body, in our mind, with our thoughts, in our heart, with our emotions, and with our spirit. We experience it holistically.

Creating and sustaining an atmosphere of silence happens through intention, focus, and practice. We intend silence to be the environment we choose to foster in our mind. Through practice, our focus naturally moves to a wealth of information and understanding that is found within the silent space. Both formal and informal practices connect us to silence. Formal practice occurs at designated times and includes activities like sitting meditation, tai chi, and journaling. Informal practices are spontaneous activities that draw our awareness to the extraordinary in our life.

Activities that focus our awareness on the Sacred in each moment create and sustain our silence. The Sacred manifests in the extraordinary or in those things, people, and relationships we hold in great reverence. Through contemplative or mindfulness practice we open our self to the Sacred. A practice may be as simple as focusing on our breath or may involve twenty to thirty minutes of sitting meditation. No matter the experience, the intent is to enter into the silence and practice being aware of the distractions but not reacting to them. We nurture silence when we are aware of and fully present in the moment.

When we are aware of our distractions through the practice of full-body listening, silence permeates our body, mind, spirit, and emotions. Perhaps we physically feel unsettled. This sensation calls for us to check in with ourselves: with what we are thinking and what emotion is triggering us. Once we have done so, we can choose either to allow these distractions to draw us away from the moment into the fog of illusion or to rest within the silence while acknowledging the distractions without reacting to them.

Silence creates the place in which we enter hyperawareness. Awareness sustains the silence. Silence and awareness empower us to move away from reacting to distraction, which then serves as a trigger for the reactions of another. Our new stance is one of responding in gentle, loving ways. The goal of any practice is to deepen our connection to silence, increase the duration of our awareness, and acknowledge but not react to our distractions. There are many contemplative or mindfulness practices that accomplish this goal.

Formal contemplative practices or mindfulness exercises create structured moments in which we focus our attention and anchor our self in the present moment. Using a focal point develops pathways into the silence. The focal point may be a word, sound, image, or the breath. Each is a means of increasing our comfort of resting in the silence, until it becomes easier to connect to the silence amid the tumult of our daily lives. When we befriend silence through practice, it becomes simple to slide quickly into this place of silence.

While some find sitting meditation helpful, others find that physical motion like walking, dancing, tai chi, qigong, and yoga bring them into the space of silence. For me, movement calms my active mind and provides the key to unlocking the gateway to the vastness of silence. Movement may be as simple as taking a walk or as intricate as a series of tai chi poses.

No matter what movement I choose, it assists me in moving into the silence. Once accessed, the silence rolls into every nook and cranny of my spirit. After the end of my physically active contemplative practice, I find it easier to maintain clarity and awareness of my distractions in my everyday moments.

Sound is another gateway to silence. Chanting and singing resonate to unlock silence's space. Experiment by listening to different types of music with different beats. After listening, be mindful of how you engage the world around you. What music invites you into a place of hyperawareness and clarity? What serves as a distraction? There are no wrong answers. The answers exist only in your connection to silence.

Other ways to enter the silence are by journaling and creating art. You do not have to be a bestselling author or a renowned artist to use these mindfulness practices. These experiences are only for your benefit. Accessing these gateways leads to increased clarity and awareness of your authentic self and your distractions. The goal is to engage in a practice that quiets your soul, acts as a balm for your weary heart, and creates welcoming awareness.

Each of our relationships provides fertile ground for nurturing our authentic self and nourishing our silence. Time spent in relationship with our self with limited distractions connects us more fully to our authentic being. Here we befriend silence and gain understanding of how to enter its calm embrace. We limit extraneous physical sound. Within fostered silence we hear what is preventing us from deeply entering and remaining in the silence.

Once we become accustomed to identifying our distractions, we gain the power of choice. Each time we choose to respond instead of react, we enter more deeply into the silence of our quiet mind. For example, we may have a headache, be hungry, or be in the presence of an irritating background noise. We may not consciously notice any of these distractions. In a cultivated quiet mind, these distractions rise to the surface of our silence. With awareness, we notice and then respond to them. Through nonattachment, we neutralize the distraction, and the path to the silence of the quiet mind is more easily trod.

When we are aware of activities that are compatible with maintaining our silence, we can choose to practice them. Silence creates an environment in which we can more easily decompress. As physical stress leaves our body, we may no longer give voice to or act upon our judgments and assumptions. We become conscious of the bombardment by stimuli. With clarity we sift through all our interactions to find where the illusions mask our authentic reality. Our awareness improves our relationship with all aspects of self—body, mind, spirit, heart.

Silence is a permeable bubble surrounding us. We choose what flows through the permeable membrane and into our life. Within this bubble of silence, we are more readily aware and fully present in the moment. Through our practice, we move past the mundane world into the extraordinary. Within the silence of our quiet mind, the world shifts into a place of adventure. Our relationships become more authentic.

With awareness we recognize clues that alert us to our illusions. These façades bar us from entering into relationship. When we let go of our illusions, we recognize the facets of our self that are true and authentic. We acknowledge to our self our hopes, dreams, and agendas. Then in the silence we discern what is authentic and what is illusion. Letting go of illusions requires humility and courage, and without these two personal attributes, contemplative relationship is not possible.

Illusions create distortions in our constellation of connections. They cloud our ability to see potential connections and connect with others in increasingly intimate ways. Without the clouds filled with illusion, we are aware of when we are backward-focused and living with regrets of the past. We notice when our attention is forward-focused with worries and dreams about the future. Living within our constellation of connections demands we live in the present moment.

When we rest in silence, we notice when our attention drifts from present time. In moments of clarity, we shift into the present moment. We let go of past- and future-focused distractions and gain a greater clarity, which invites us into meaningful connection with our self, the Sacred, others, and creation.

Within the environment of silence, we identify what is true and recognize what is illusion. We also discover and access the limitless well of unconditional love and grace. We courageously connect to our divine spark and become a conduit of compassion. As we share love and compassion with our self, we first begin to heal the cracks of our wounded soul. Like a piece of raku pottery that has been mended, we become a stronger vessel in which our silence resides. Through this strengthened vessel, we enter into mindful relationship.

Self-love, self-compassion, and self-acceptance are vital to developing and sustaining this place of silence. When we love our self unconditionally, we release old hurts and forgive our perceived transgressions. Through self-compassion, we gain the strength to humbly accept the fallibility that is our humanity. Through self-acceptance, we move toward what is authentic and let go of illusion.

With self-acceptance, we become more courageous. Courage propels us on the slow, and at times arduous, journey of transformation. By courageously accepting our self, we realize we are part of the circle of creation. Through this connection, we rest in a silence in which we are never alone. We are nourished in ways that soothe our soul and heal us.

When we begin the process of healing our self, we are capable of entering into other contemplative relationships. An authentic relationship with our self is the foundation of fulfilling relationships with others. When we recognize our true face, we gain the skills to co-create the authentic face of other relationships.

Within silence we connect to our primary relationship, the one with our self. Thomas Merton reminds us of the importance of knowing our self: "If we think our mask is our true face, we will protect it with fabrications even at the cost of violating our truth."[8] Violating our truth prevents us from connection with others. Casting aside our illusions, we stand in our authenticity.

Unless we foster silence, our ability to sustain other relationships is impaired. An invisible barrier exists between our self and others that can be made visible and dismantled only through clarity. The journey begins with the relationship with oneself, but all relationships empower us to learn our life lessons, discover the grace of interdependence, and live with joy. We share unconditional love and compassion found in the reservoir of silence.

Silence gives us the flexibility to move into clarity, allowing relationships to evolve in ways they are meant to, whether that deepens connections or not. When relationships end, we must look intently at all four aspects of the relationship. Through this examination we find ways to heal in the physical, emotional, mental, and spiritual realms.

When my marriage ended in divorce, it was not just a dissolution on paper. I intentionally ended the relationship on physical, spiritual, mental, and emotional levels. I realized that my connection to his divine spark might never be extinguished. This was not necessary to shift the nature of the relationship. He will always be part of my constellation of connections.

Over our life our constellation of connections continues to grow. Our divine spark connects with the divine sparks of many, including all of creation. When a relationship shifts, we are still connected. As long as we are connected, there is potential for deep, and at times wordless, communication. Engaging in communion in relationships roots them firmly in our mind.

Creating a Constellation of Connections

Sit quietly. Focus on your breathing. Allow it to naturally flow in and out. Don't shift your inhale/exhale. Just notice. Rest in the silence of your quiet mind. Notice with all of your senses how it feels.

Now reflect upon and respond to the following:

- How do you best create silence?
- How do you best enter silence?
- How do you best nurture silence?

Reenter the silence with the answers. Name your distractions.

- How do these distractions help you create and sustain illusions?
- Name some of those illusions.

What contemplative practices help you identify distractions and release the illusions?

Chapter 6

The Quiet Mind

Silence, the inky night sky, is the milieu we use to minimize the potential effects of distractions that overwhelm us. Within silence we are aware of the distractions. Through the clarity fostered in silence, it only takes seconds to craft a response that neutralizes any trigger and empowers the relationship. A simple comment from a person may trigger our defenses. Through full-body listening, we feel our physical body clenching and hear the words of a potential reaction. Aware of what is being triggered, we breathe into our silence and choose a response instead of a reaction. When regularly cultivated, silence enhances our ability to distinguish between distractions and authentic information. Through our quiet mind we choose to express the self authentically, humbly, and with courage.

Deep within the silent mind rests the ground of our being, a place of safety and security. In this place, we cannot hide from our authentic self. Our illusions manifest in ways that cannot be ignored or misinterpreted. When we live in courageous awareness in each evolving moment, we identify the roots of our illusions and take steps to purge them from the ground of our being.

Within this ground we develop and sustain a relationship with our authentic self. We identify our wounded spirit and draw intentionally upon the bottomless well of our self-compassion. On this healing journey to wholeness, we authentically connect with others in contemplative relationship. This is possible through the quiet mind. Through our quiet mind, the clarity of silence trickles into each of our actions, words, and thoughts.

Within our quiet mind we access our internal monologue and judgments, assumptions, and beliefs. Our thoughts stem from our judgments, assumptions, and beliefs. When we rest within the silence of our quiet mind, we clearly hear that internal monologue. We recognize how our personal reality is based upon our internal monologue and accept that our unique point of view may be different from that of another. We acknowledge that our reality may not be accurate.

By listening to this often ignored inner voice, we gain more clarity about how we have personally constructed our reality. The jumbled tumult of our world becomes a more easily discerned pattern. We identify what is illusion and how we have created it with distractions. Resting in our quiet mind, we gain greater understanding of how to navigate the obstacles of distraction. Through this navigation we deepen our connection to our authentic self.

Becoming an objective observer within the pockets of silence, we formulate responses. In these spaces our judgments, assumptions, and beliefs become visible. Using the 4nons (nonattachment, nonjudgment, nondefensiveness, nonviolence), we cannot honestly ignore them. The connection between distractions and our thoughts, words, and actions becomes apparent. We understand how the roots of our thoughts, words, and actions hinder us. Each trigger that we successfully master gives us the tools to respond to other triggers. Responses strengthen relationships; reactions tear them down. We change the way we relate to others.

Each of us can identify a person, event, or circumstance guaranteed to throw us into reaction. Often without thought and sometimes after an argument with our self, we break through our silence. In those moments we react to life's tumult. We react to another's words or actions. Later when we rest in the silence of our quiet mind, we become aware of the friction caused by our reactions. With this self-awareness, we can soothe our inner turmoil and strengthen our ability to respond.

At one of my jobs, I clashed with the bookkeeper. It seemed that no matter in what format I gave the information to her, there was something wrong with it. I found myself becoming more and more stressed and making more mistakes. I felt targeted. When I asked for clarity about how we could work together, she pointed out my character flaws. In retrospect, I have found many better ways to shift from reactionary behavior to response, but I was seldom able to do that in real time.

Through reflection we probe why we are habitually reactive in certain circumstances. Reflection empowers us to identify the pattern of reaction and realize its consequences. We understand that reactions drag us out of our silence and shatter the silence of another. The reverberation of each reaction is far reaching. Reflection is a key tool in creating intimate relationships. Our quiet mind is the place of reflection.

The quiet mind is the home of the objective observer. Within the silence we practice the 4nons by not clinging to or casting off illusions, not judging others, not defending behaviors, and not lashing out violently. By adopting the stance of the objective observer, we identify what lies at the root of our reactions.

We might identify a judgment we have about another or a situation. As an objective observer, we do not desperately need for that judgment to be accurate. We are nonattached and choose not to react from the judgment (nonjudgement). Noticing but not defending our thoughts, we modify any violent thoughts, whether they are directed to our self or another. Through the 4nons, we are an objective observer who discovers the root of our illusion.

Often that root is fear. Fear exaggerates the illusions created by our judgements, assumptions, and beliefs. But acknowledging and accepting the roots of our reactions is scary. It takes honesty and humility to accept those parts of our self that are false. Courage is our companion as we make changes to banish our reactions to triggers.

Our quiet mind is the place to explore our authentic self and to deepen the relationship with the self. In this ground of our being, we are able to peer deeply and intently into the reality of our life. Humility requires that we gently and compassionately identify what is truly us and what needs to change in order to create authenticity.

Courage is the force behind our transformation to our best, truest self. Courage impels us in this intimate self-appraisal to separate the chaff from the wheat. We name what is illusion and what is really us. With integrity we move along the path of transformation while blessing the lessons that are birthed from recognizing illusion.

Within the quiet mind are opportunities to flourish. As the dark blanket of silence wraps comfort around us, we listen courageously and are ready to learn. We question the impact of a person or situation on us and how we have impacted another. Through full-body listening we acknowledge the scars some encounters have left while being careful not to blame or allow anger's roots to further burrow within us. Silence allows us to uproot these weeds.

In sharing compassion with our self and others, we better understand how these encounters have formed our own reality and how we interact with others in the world. Through methodical reflection and introspection, we create a plan of intent and action. When we act upon the strategies within the plan, personal and relational transformation occurs.

With awareness we connect with silence. For example, I once had a supervisor with whom I had a very strained relationship. Often I would be paranoid that I had overstepped yet another invisible boundary. One day I passed her in the hallway. Neither of us acknowledged the other. When I returned to my office, I wondered why she did not say hello. Most of the afternoon I spent in a place of backward focus as I ruminated over the perceived slight.

That evening after my son had gone to sleep, I rested in the silence. As I lay swaddled in silence's safety, I realized that although she had not initiated a greeting, neither had I. In that moment my illusion that she was the ogre who was out to get me became clear. My fear-filled behavior was based upon my judgment of the roles each of us had assumed in my reality.

During the next hallway passing, I initiated the greeting. As I looked at her, I saw her entire body shift. She smiled. Over the course of the next several months, our relationship shifted from adversarial to cordial. This was the beginning of releasing the mistrust we had harbored for too long. Our respect for each other grew. When I left the job several years later, that supervisor gave me one of the best references I had ever received.

The transformation of an external relationship occurs only when we begin the arduous process of transformation of self. Authentic transformation requires that we foster the silence of our quiet mind. Attending to our internal monologue is only possible with clarity—an outcome of resting in silence.

With clarity, we are better able to discern the validity of our judgments and assumptions. Not all judgments and assumptions are harmful or invalid. Some judgments are necessary for the survival of our authentic self. Understanding which judgments are valid and which are not gives us power of choice. We can remain mired in an illusory relationship or move through the tumult of our private conversations and into deeper relationship.

Internal monologue, monkey mind, and spinning top are a few of the many ways to describe the conversation we have with our self. Even when we are unaware of this voice, it is our constant companion. At times we are aware of the internal monologue. At other times the murmurs lie just below our awareness. Yet, at other times, we detect a dull whisper that we hear but cannot quite grasp the meaning. This commentary continuously runs in the background, impacting all of our interactions. With awareness, we enter silence, listen, and decipher its meaning.

Resting in silence is key to increasing awareness of the monologue. In silence we are in the moment. Being fully present allows us to choose how our internal monologue impacts our words and actions. By cultivating an awareness of our internal monologue, we can choose how and if we are distracted. This sifting through our distractions is the first step in making a conscious choice of how we are in relationship.

Listening to our internal monologue while resting in the silence may reveal surprises. We make judgments and form assumptions often without being aware. By listening to our internal monologue, we discover the basis of our beliefs, recognize how we are triggered, and see the patterns that result from our reactions. This understanding provides the foundation of response.

I have often found it difficult to be in relationship with someone who is conservative. (Even as I write this, I recognize that I am judging and labeling.) My conversations with them are often stilted. I find myself unsure of how I can form the questions that lead to better understanding of their worldview. The interaction often feels unbalanced. When I rest within the silence of my quiet mind, I am aware of how my assumptions about the word "conservative" prevent me from seeing beyond the differences in our beliefs and finding common ground.

During one conversation, my awareness was astute enough for me to see beyond labels I had imposed. Honestly and humbly I owned my many judgments and assumptions about the other person. I was shocked by the chasm of separation I had created between the person and me. As I rested in the silence, I began to dredge up other assumptions and judgments. Our conversation was no longer combative.

I used to believe that "liberals" were more open to the ideas of others. Conversely, I believed that "conservatives" were more likely to be closed to the ideas of others. What a surprise it was for me to discover that it was less the belief system and more the willingness of the individual to enter into relationship with another that created a pathway of openness.

Through this personal and very intimate examination, a bridge extended across the chasm. I hope this bridge leads me to find common ground the next time I enter into conversation with someone whose views are different from mine. This way of interacting reminds me that being in relationship means resting together in the common ground to gain understanding—not a place of agreement but one of respect.

While we may have very different beliefs, the core of each one of us is similar. Each of us strives to find a way to live our soul purpose. Very few of us intentionally looks for ways to hurt or be harmful. When we begin with this commonality, we move beyond our differences and discover ways to support one another. Silence creates the space in which we examine our own heart and find ways to reach out to someone we view as very dissimilar.

When we embrace the other with unconditional love and grace, the paradigm shifts. We enter a reality in which we look beyond differences and consciously accept our similarities as a means of reaching common ground. While on common ground our objective is to understand the other. We lose the desire to be right and place blame. Although neither party may change his or her core beliefs, a sense of respect between parties grows. In this place we are truly intimate. In this intimacy we form contemplative relationship.

The more we rest in silence and consciously listen to our internal monologue, the easier it becomes to bi-listen. Bi-listening is consciously and intentionally being aware of the internal mono-logue and the external dialogues. The intent of this way of listening is to connect our thoughts with our interactions. When we bi-lis-ten, we have opportunities to see patterns created by our thoughts, words, and actions. With this recognition comes the power of choice. We choose which patterns need to be rescripted. We choose to connect intimately in our relationships.

Another benefit of creating an environment of silence is increased resiiency. With awareness comes flexibility; with flexibili-ty we are less likely to react from a place of fear or scarcity. Instead, within the silence, time expands. In this expansive place, we notice the trigger and choose to respond or react to it. Within our silence, we navigate the obstacles with increased clarity.

The words of our internal monologue become clear. From this clarity follows a more thoughtful response to the world. We shape our external dialogue in gentle, compassionate ways. Our quiet mind births a heartfelt response. We minimize our reactions. Through resiliency and awareness, we have the option of choice. We use this option when connecting to the external.

Creating a Constellation of Connections

Sit quietly. Focus on your breathing. Do not try to shift your breath. Allow it to naturally flow in and out. Just notice. Become aware of your internal monologue.

- Spend some time listening to your internal monologue. (You may want to set a timer for five minutes.)
- Next, write down your impressions of the monologue. Consider using a narrative, outline, bullet points, or some other way to help you gain clarity of what you heard.
- Reflect upon what you have written.
- Choose two or three of your thoughts to focus on.
- Name the judgments and assumptions that lie at the roots of each thought.
- Name your beliefs that are the basis for your thoughts. For example, if you are thinking about a conversation, what do you believe about the interactions? What do you believe is the basis of both you and your partner's words?
- Ask yourself what is an illusion and what is authentic. Are you making assumptions that are not true and based upon your triggers? If so, name them.
- Name your personal reality.—how do you see the world? Is it true and accurate or based on illusion?
- What parts of your reality are accurate? How does illusion form your reality?
- Find ways to rescript those illusions that prevent you from living authentically.

Chapter 7

Start at the Beginning

Through the mystery and beauty of silence, our connections burn brightly. When we live in deep awareness, we see the connections. Without hyperawareness, we miss opportunities for relationship. As silence permeates our essence, we wake up. We become fully aware of and fully invested in each action we take. Our relationships become contemplative.

While it may seem that we are free to easily change our behavior from reaction to response, we may underestimate how deeply our path is rutted. We may misjudge how difficult it is to fill the ruts and create a new path. After over half a century in relationship with family, it is easy to fall into certain roles. No matter if one of us has shifted into another way of relating, it is almost impossible to see beyond the previous patterns. These patterns have caused ruts that are almost impossible to climb out of.

Each rut represents a pattern that is deeply carved by reactions and responses to our thoughts and the words and actions of our self and others. Patterns can be beneficial, destructive, or neutral. When we are able to respond to another in loving, gentle ways, no matter what the provocation, we are maintaining a beneficial pattern. A destructive pattern would be to react to another based upon our assumptions and judgments or the previous behavior of others. We may find our self responding almost without thought. Smiling at a neighbor or checking out at the grocery store may be neither beneficial nor destructive.

During those moments when we are unaware, we become lost in the fog of reactionary illusion. We react again and again in harmful and hurtful ways. It may seem that we have no choice but to react. Our vision may be so cluttered by illusions, we believe that the only viable choice is to react to the fears triggered by our assumptions and judgments. As we deepen the ruts that have become a pattern, we see no way to reroute our pattern and thus enter more deeply into contemplative relationship.

Through awareness, we peel back the layers of illusion. During the assessment that is part of our awareness, we question what is real and identify how illusions may feel different from truth. This is the beginning of reforming our patterns. The process of identifying patterns and reframing may be slow and frustrating. Through patience and honesty, illusions can be released, habits repatterned, and our authentic nature aligned with the ground of our being. Our relationships benefit from this awareness and reflection.

It is easy to become discouraged by how we have placed the same barriers over and over again in different relationships. Courage and integrity help us identify nonworking patterns and forge a new path. Our integrity invites us to name the ways we unknowingly sabotage connections. Courage asks that we seek alternatives to our reactions in an effort to break down the walls that divide us. Through courage and integrity, we build welcoming connections with others. Creating new ways of connecting is not simple, but it is very rewarding.

Connecting with others in contemplative relationship begins first by understanding our self. On this path of living contemplatively we are no longer able to delude our self into accepting what is false. Our integrity compels us to cultivate words and actions that draw us into deeper, more honest connection. Our actions may very well spark a contemplative response in our partner.

With clarity nurtured in silence, we accept full responsibility for our role in all our connections with others, the Sacred, and all of creation. We acknowledge the obstacles created by our distractions. Our intent is to consciously dismantle each obstacle through compassionate response. The longer we rest in silence, the more clarity we gain about the cause of each obstacle. We use the understanding that comes from clarity to dismantle the façades that prevent us from living authentically. Creating the illusion of strength with no weakness is one façade that we create. By showing our vulnerability, we remove this façade. Each façade we relinquish allows our authentic self to connect honestly with others.

When we become an objective observer, we step outside of our illusions and perceive the impact our judgments and assumptions have on others and our relationships. Perceiving the impact is only the beginning. With clarity we seek ways to minimize or negate previous hurt while developing new, non-reactive ways of connecting. With awareness and clarity, each interaction with our self helps us better understand who we are. Knowing our self is the basis of any authentic relationship, be it with our self or another, the Sacred, or any aspect of creation.

As we continue to release our illusions, we recognize, when we are present, the judgments and assumptions that we make. The key is to be aware of them while not being distracted by them. With this awareness, we are able to choose words and actions that represent our true, best self instead of our illusions and fears.

Awareness of our distractions is vital to dialoguing with others. Using this dialogue is two-fold. We articulate without words through nonverbal cues and with words. If we allow our judgment of how a person looks or what they wear to be reflected in our body language or facial expressions, the other person may close down. In the same way, if our words are judgmental or critical, the other may retreat. Relationship aborted.

Resting in the silence to gain a greater understanding of our distractions enables us to choose to respond instead of react. Our internal monologue is deeply rooted in our soul essence. Our external dialogue grows from roots twined in our soul essence as it invites connection. A strong foundation of relationship with self strengthens the connection with others and opens us fully to exploring the depth of that connection. This translates into greater relationship durability.

A strong foundation is built on more than our awareness of distractions. Silence creates a safe place in which we conduct a personal inventory in order to discover how we can live in humility and with integrity. We name what resonates at the ground of our being. Courageously we identify what prevents us from living with integrity. The light of silence shines upon any misconceptions we may be under.

Calling upon our humility, we embrace what is false. We shower our misconceptions with compassion. We let go of what is not truly ours. Finally, we repattern our life script in ways that reflect the ground of our being. We foster authentic relationships with others by fashioning a more true relationship with our self.

This path of awareness and transformation begins within the silence of our quiet mind. Here our foundation is strengthened. Silence becomes a constant companion. This permeable bubble of silence surrounds us. As we grow accustomed to resting inside it, silence becomes a constant, intangible comfort. We have a sustainable backdrop for contemplative relationships to thrive.

When we venture into the world, we are encased by this bubble but not contained by it. Our interactions are enhanced by silence. We discover a growing clarity. We are able to see past the many distractions that bombard us in each moment. We choose what flows into the permeable membrane and then into our reality. Our viable choice is to enter into contemplative relationship.

This bubble, like all of life, is not static. It is permeable and has no definable boundaries. Our intent is that it be filled with compassion and be representative of our authentic self. Depending upon the day or the situation, it may become more porous and filled with illusions. We lose awareness, distractions rush in, and we react. When this happens we return to the silence in our quiet mind. While we may not be able to change our previous reactions, we can prevent future ones from causing more damage.

We recognize that although we carry it with us, silence does not belong to us. It is living and organic. Like the night sky, it flows between each sparking ember. Silence swaddles us. Through silence we are soothed and are encouraged to let go of petty distractions, choosing to respond instead of react. Within silence, two individuals become partners and form a relationship.

Although each of us creates an individual bubble of silence, this bubble is permeable. The bubbles merge if only for a moment during each interaction. Within the merging of silence, compassion flares in our divine spark. This energy creates a connection of communion between partners in the relationship.

When we enter into relationships with others, our silence twines with theirs. This twined silence is vital to connection. We cannot paint a picture unless we have a canvas. The twining silence forms the canvas of relationship. Against the background of silence, we notice each potential interaction. We identify what prevents us from entering into a relationship and what assists in strengthening the connection. When we act upon this knowing, we strengthen sustainable relationships. Listening within the silence guides us ever deeper into connection.

As an intuitive mentor, I meet with individuals wanting to find clarity in their current life situation. Before a conversation, I spend time in the silence preparing to listen with my entire being. We both enter a space of shared silence as we listen to one another. Without the silence, my intuition would not lead me to pertinent information. I would be unable to phrase my questions in ways that would bring responses from my clients. My client gains important insights for the journey. All the result of shared silence.

We are aware of the role of reverence in relationship. Reverence requires that we look beyond façades and illusions in order to discover what lies at the authentic core of another. We respect the other for who they are even if we do not understand their beliefs or agree with them. When we bring this deep form of respect into dialogue, we offer the other honesty and trust. Through reverence we are open to receiving the gifts inherent in the connection. Reverence empowers us to understand without judgment or defensive behavior.

Silence sets the path for our relationships to flourish. In silence we sit with our emotional triggers and gain clarity. Within this space we choose between reacting and responding. We see the twinkling presence of others and create the path to connect with them. Silence creates an ambiance of safety. Within this security and with courage, we explore paths that draw us closer to authenticity and farther from our illusions.

Silence is the place where we see clearly and choose to respond or react to distractions. While a distraction may arise from our emotions, it has many other faces. Anything that draws our attention from the present moment is a distraction. Distractions may be benign. The ringing of a phone or a knock on a door draws our focus away from the moment.

More than a physical cessation of noise, silence is an environment in which we identify our distractions and illusions and step more fully into our place of authenticity—the ground of our being. At the ground of our being, we rest in relationship with our self and nourish our divine spark. Within the silence, our divine spark connects to the divine sparks of others. We recognize a common ground of being that is alive with connection.

Contemplative relationships begin in silence. In this environment, we nurture our awareness of self and of how we contribute to the function and dysfunction of our relationships. Understanding self requires the energy of compassion emanating from our divine spark. This energy of compassion flows to the parts of us that are wounded. Compassion lifts us past the hurt and into a place of healing. Through the healing of self we become a healing presence to others.

Relationships are formed and sustained within joint silence. Pathways of relationship are strengthened through the deepest form of communication, communion. We choose a more intimate, deeper way of connecting when we engage in communion. This type of communication requires full-body listening and compassionate response. Without silence it would be difficult to share compassion and to communicate on deep, sustainable levels. The journey begins with silence but requires compassion and communion to transform connections into contemplative relationships.

Creating a Constellation of Connections

Sit quietly. Focus on your breathing. Do not try to shift your breathing. Allow it to naturally flow in and out. Just notice. Become aware of who you are at the center of your being. Spend time in reflection as you discern what is an illusion and what is your authentic self.

- Name those parts that represent who you truly are.
- Identify the illusions that separate you from your authentic self.

What encourages you to enter more deeply into relationship? What illusions create barriers?

How did illusion damage the connection you had with your relationship partner?

Reflect upon a relationship. How did your authenticity and your illusions help form your connection?

Night sky = silence

Chapter 8

Compassion Is...Our Divine Spark

Within each of us glows an ember. Carved from the Sacred, we carry this divine spark from the conception of our spirit throughout our existence. This divine spark is aglow and pulses with our compassion. We share, we receive, we connect—all with the power of the compassion of our divine spark. We access this compassion through silence and by nurturing our contemplative spirit.

Through awareness we adopt a contemplative stance. We focus on the awareness of the Sacred or the extraordinary in our life. In this awareness we wake to the extraordinary and are alive to the possibility of connection. In this place of intentional presence, we form our connections with other people, the Sacred, and all aspects of creation. These connections are filled with compassion and unconditional love.

Opportunities to birth and grow our constellation of connections occur within each aspect and facet of our life. In those moments when our focus is no longer in the moment, we miss opportunities to connect with compassion. When we are present, our focus is on life unfolding instead of being disturbed by planning our grocery list, rehashing an upsetting situation from earlier in the day, or planning our dream vacation. At times, being present means that we are planning a grocery list or reflecting upon a previous situation. Being in the moment means we are fully focused on what is happening at that time. Connecting intimately happens by setting aside mundane distractions and focusing on the extraordinary unfolding in the moment.

Compassion asks us to be aware of how we are perpetrators of hurt. We notice how we form connections and how we fracture them. Our actions and words can twine the strands of another more deeply into our sparks or fray the fragile connections. The light of compassion shines upon our motives and agendas. Self-compassion provides the courage to admit when we have slipped into inauthenticity. Then we have the strength to move away from the illusions and rest more firmly in our truth.

Through self-compassion, we are able to identify where we intentionally hurt and where we thoughtlessly harm. Connecting to our spark of compassion is simple. Our life at times is messy and angst-producing. When we connect to our spark, we are flooded with self-compassion, angst evaporates, and we find the energy to share compassion with others.

Self-compassion is the necessary kindling for compassion that is shared outward. Each time our compassion sparks inward, we fill the well of our compassion. Well filled, we are better able to channel the power of compassion along our relationship connections. Through these connections, we trigger a burst of companion compassion in others.

Compassion is simply defined as a desire to alleviate suffering. For Thomas Merton, "Compassion teaches me that my brother and I are one. That if I love my brother, then my love benefits my own life as well, and if I hate my brother and seek to destroy him, I seek to destroy myself also."[8] When we alleviate suffering while being aware, we create our own definition of compassion. We discover our personal, lived experience of compassion and how it empowers the divine sparks of others through our connections. When compassion becomes our lived experience, every moment is an opportunity to alleviate suffering.

Without living with awareness, we would be enclosed in a impermeable bubble of isolation. When we are in this self-imposed isolation, we are unable to intimately connect. We do not recognize the deep suffering in the world around us that is often a mirror of our own suffering. Engaging compassion is a communal experience in which we alleviate suffering in others, not only for their sakes but also to bring us peace.

Our many expressions of compassion are as unique as we are. As the ember of compassion glows in the ground of our being, we uniquely share our expression of compassion. While we often share it in ways that are habitual, at other times our sharing may be spontaneous and/or somewhere just outside of our comfort zone. Through awareness, we notice the flare of need. Regardless of our level of comfort, when we respond with compassion, our relationships radiate with unconditional love and happiness.

Friday mornings have become my grocery shopping time. Often individuals with less mobility are purchasing foodstuffs. One morning, upon recognizing my unease at how slow the fellow shopper in front of me was moving, I asked her if I could help place groceries on the conveyer belt. She was grateful since she had difficulty bending. Our conversation gave me renewed energy to work alone for the rest of the day. A spontaneous act of compassion returned to me, giving me a more positive outlook.

Expressions of compassion are limitless. Compassion manifests as a listening ear or a gentle hug. It may be offering tangible support like making a donation. Compassion may be a response to an individual or be shared with a community. Any act that is the result of our intent to alleviate suffering is a compassionate one. Each compassion-filled act contributes to a heart-centered lived experience. Within this way of living we sustain our constellation of connections.

We share our divine sparks and twine our compassion with others in ways that empower interdependence. Alleviating suffering is not about enabling or becoming codependent. Compassion calls us to stand in solidarity with others while encouraging them to shed the chains of suffering. Removing these chains may not be without pain. With compassion we gently accompany the other as they discover how to shed their chains.

Shedding suffering may produce angst. When we let go of those things, people, and situations that cause suffering, we create a void. In this place of absence, angst may creep in. We may find our self stuck in a loop of thoughts. We may wonder when the next bout of suffering will occur. Resting in the silence and practicing additional self-compassion encourages us to release the angst and be in peace.

First we are compassionate to our self, and then we encourage others to be gently self-compassionate. Without self-compassion, our ability to alleviate the suffering of another is severely limited. This internal flow of compassion minimizes our fatigue and provides the energy for us to respond to others with compassion.

Compassion is heart-centered. At times I find no logical or rational reason to share compassion. In fact, I could present a sound argument for walking away. But, as Tibetan Buddhist monk Matthieu Ricard said during a presentation at the Louisville, Kentucky, Festival of Faith in May 2014, "Compassion is not a reward for good behavior." Compassion is not a political affair but a deep-seated yearning to enter into solidarity and be with another who suffers. There is no hidden agenda when we share compassion.

I envision compassion as a watercolor wash of rose quartz that swirls within our self. It cannot be contained within the bubble of our existence. When we are aware, the sparks of compassion escape into the world. Once in the world, compassion mends, heals, and strengthens our connections. It twines with others and completes the circuit as it returns to us. The circle is not finished but is energized to run the cycle an infinite number of times.

The practice of self-compassion strengthens our primary relationship—the relationship with self. We may be overwhelmed by fatigue and suffer burnout. This happens more than we admit because, unfortunately, we are masters at ignoring or minimizing our personal suffering. We may judge our suffering and needs as not important. Being authentic means we practice self-compassion.

Through awareness we recognize our festering wounds. With this awareness, we turn our compassion within. Even when we believe we do not have time to rest in silence, it is imperative that we find time. Silence increases our awareness of fatigue and the power to rejuvenate our compassionate presence. In silence we can access our compassion more easily. By recognizing and acknowledging our own suffering, we begin to understand how to heal those wounded parts of our self. Compassion is our companion healer on the journey to wholeness.

On this journey we identify the parts of our self that are not true. These illusions may provide a false sense of security or we may fear the void that will appear if we let them go. Compassion coupled with courage creates the gateway through which we let go of the illusions. Courage and compassion empower us to meet the fear of the void head on and to prepare for what will fill it. Letting go of the illusions that cause suffering frees space to live a fully connected life. Letting go of our suffering strengthens our connection with our authentic self.

At times, we may feel crushed under the weight of our suffering. We may not feel worthy of living without the suffering. Self-compassion's companion, courage, brings us to a place of forgiveness, even when we feel that we have perpetrated untenable acts. Self-compassion is the tool of forgiveness. With this balm we let go the behavior that triggered suffering. We dress our wounds. In this healing space we more easily address our suffering and its causes. Compassion brings us to the realization that nothing is unforgivable.

Forgiveness requires courage. With courage we forge the path through which compassion flows. With curious daring, we peer into our newly revealed self to discover ways to undergo transformation. Only when we are transforming to an authentic self do we connect with others in contemplative relationship. We gain the strength to nurture compassion, the spirit of our heart. We selflessly direct compassion outward. Our holistic expression of compassion is external and internal. The never-ending cycle continues.

We became a part of this cycle at the conception of our spirit when we received a shard carved from the Sacred. Jewish mysticism calls this the divine spark. From the spark, our essence flares. This ember holds the spark of divine compassion. Divine compassion fuels our compassion. Our life force is wrapped in compassion and shared with all of creation.

Compassion is multidirectional. We receive compassion from the Sacred and return it during prayer. We share it with others and all of creation. When our heart is open, compassion returns to us tenfold. With each act of compassion, we blow gently on our divine spark. It glows more brightly and warmer. This compassion flows through the strands that connect to the Sacred. Our relationship with the Sacred deepens; the spark twinkles and the Sacred is reflected brightly in us.

The brightly shining light of compassion urges us to respond. We respond, and the light shining brightly outward impacts our relationships with others. Inward and outward compassion draws us more deeply into relationship. We accept more opportunities to connect and enter deeply into relationship. Our constellation strengthens.

Within us our compassion glows. It emanates from us and reaches out to more than the humans in our sphere of influence. Through our awareness, we shower compassion on other sentient beings. What does it mean to act compassionately with others in creation? Perhaps it is a cuddle with a frenetic animal companion or the capture and release of an insect that has found its way indoors. Sustainable living might be the answer for some. Compassion as a lived experience means we discern how we share compassion. There is no wrong way to share it.

When compassion becomes our lived experience, we respond to the cues and triggers in the world around us in our own unique way. We define our self and our view of reality through the ways our intent to be compassionate manifests in our actions. We are mindful of the ways that our action is not aligned with our intent.

We are not static beings. With our dynamic, flexible way of living, we discover how we are called to compassion. This way evolves as we practice compassionate action. As we share it, we live a heart-centered life that invites us to live always seeking and accepting opportunities to be compassionate. Contemplative relationship requires that we actively embrace a compassionate life.

Compassion is defined as an alleviation of suffering or suffering with. These definitions merely serve as the means to take the first steps on our journey with compassion. Through an ongoing practice of RI^2 (reflection, introspection, and integration), we discover many ways compassion accompanies us and how we are asked to accompany it. We move away from reacting from fear and toward responding with our heart.

With honestly, humility, and courage, we identify and question the behaviors that are, at the very least, neutral and, at the worst, harmful. We choose actions that more fully reflect our compassionate nature. Sinking into the marrow of our being, compassion becomes a core part of our self. It guides us toward unconditional love and steers us away from hurtful behavior.

RI^2 is a means of discovering what compassion asks of us in the moment and how to respond intuitively to that request. Each time we respond, we rest firmly in the heart of compassion. Within this space we attend to the suffering of our self and others. We discover what lies in the center of our spirit: our compassionate heart.

Creating a Constellation of Connections

Before beginning your day, practice this visualization:

Sit quietly. Focus on your breathing. Allow it to naturally flow in and out. Don't shift your inhale/exhale. Just notice. As you focus on your breath, it will naturally even and become balanced. Become aware of who you are at the center of your being.

Envision that the air around you is filled with compassion… a pale rose color…breathe in compassion…see it flow throughout your body filling you up…compassion flows from your physical body in a bubble that surrounds you…this is a permeable bubble… you choose what goes out…you choose what comes in…now envision that your bubble brushes up against others as you share compassion…receive compassion from others.

Envision that the air around you is filled with compassion. . . a pale rose color . . . Breathe in compassion . . . See it flow throughout your body, filling you up . . . Compassion flows from your physical body in a bubble that surrounds you . . . This is a permeable bubble . . . You choose what goes out . . . You choose what comes in . . . Now envision that your bubble brushes up against others as you share compassion . . . Receive compassion from others.

Be aware of the bubble throughout your day. Allow it to become a part of your compassion sharing.

At the end of your day, reflect upon your interactions. Did this visualization shift how you responded and reacted to others and to situations in your world? If so, how?

Chapter 9

The Heart of Compassion

Compassion is an affair of the heart. It is a loving response to suffering. Sharing compassion is often not the result of a logical, intellectual rumination. True compassion is shared with anyone and every thing regardless of perceived worthiness. Listening to our quiet mind, we share compassion simply to alleviate the suffering.

How we share this healing presence is unique to each of us. There is no manual or how-to guide for compassionate action. The desire to alleviate suffering is intuitive and heart-centered. The more we respond to our nudges to be compassionate, the more spontaneous we are in alleviating suffering.

At times our thought to be compassionate is two steps behind our action. Have you ever found yourself consoling a grieving friend? Helping a stranger without thought? Perhaps you moved into action before you realized you even meant to help another. At any moment of shared compassion our spark flares and the spirit, will, and feeling of the heart combine to become compassionate action.

Thomas Merton, near the end of his life, in May 1968, mentioned these three aspects of the heart. He wrote, "Attention: Concentration of the spirit in the heart. Vigilance: Concentration of the will in the heart. Sobriety: Concentration of feeling in the heart."[9] I believe these heart aspects are integral to living a compassion-filled life. For Merton, attention or awareness resides in the Spirit of the Heart. Vigilance or motivation is the Will of the Heart. Sobriety or intentional manifestation is the Feeling of the Heart.

These heart-centered aspects twine into a cord on which the spark of compassion flares.

These three aspects—spirit, will, and feeling—twine together to form a triad braid that strengthens our connections to others. When they are a guiding force in each relationship, we discover an ever-deepening intimacy by moving beyond superficial interaction. We see the other with our entire being and respond from the ground of our being. As partners in relationship, we act upon our yearning to understand what lies beneath the façade of superficial relationship.

By approaching our connections in a heart-centered way, we take advantage of opportunities to banish the illusions that trigger our suffering. Through a courageous heart, we seek to understand the root of our judgments and assumptions. Through our understanding, we gain the power to become alleviators of suffering. Compassion is no longer something we share only with those deeply connected to us. The suffering of others, even the intimate stranger, becomes a magnet that draws our compassionate response.

The Spirit of the Heart is the place of our unspoken intent and our desire to be a member of community. It emanates from the ground of our being, the origin of unconditional love's flow. The Spirit of the Heart flows from the well of compassion. The well is never empty. It fills through living authentically and honestly as we share love unconditionally. We gain clarity and understanding of how distractions direct our words and actions. Within the reservoir of the spirit lies our ability to speak with loving honesty.

Through the Spirit of the Heart our wounded soul is calmed; we no longer lash out in hurtful ways. With hyperawareness of our thoughts we see the non-helpful patterns we have developed over our lifetime. The Spirit of the Heart guides us in reframing our patterns.

Perhaps instead of blurting out a hurtful word, we choose to remain silent. This is the beginning of repatterning. We notice the different ways feedback from reactions and responses manifests in our body. Through the Spirit of the Heart, we rest in this grounded place of love and bask in self-compassion. We befriend our authentic self. All other relationships benefit.

Engaging the Spirit of the Heart creates a more intentional connection with the Sacred. Remember, all relationships are a triad. Strong connections to our self and the Sacred assure the strongest, most intimate connection possible with others. Our divine spark is energized and replenished through this relationship. Our connections with others and all of creation strengthen.

Returning again and again to the spirit's reservoir empowers us to see the extraordinary in the world. Approaching the world as extraordinary releases the angst. We see possibilities where only the improbable existed before. We repattern our thoughts, words, and actions. We create a spiral that alleviates suffering and shares unconditional love.

The Spirit of the Heart washes away the murkiness that obscures our illusions. As we peer through the muck, we honestly identify when we act less than impeccably. We no longer are able to excuse or justify any self-righteous, harmful behavior. The catalysts of reaction no longer have power over us. We see them for what they are—distractions that prevent us from connecting deeply and meaningfully. We draw upon our heart's reservoir and befriend our distractions. We lovingly respond to the sources of our distractions. We lose our desire to react in harsh ways. Compassion becomes the only viable response.

It takes time, energy, and self-compassion to create new patterns of response. Our desire to react to perceived hurts doesn't disappear overnight. Through the Spirit of the Heart, we notice the peace and joy that permeate us when we respond. Over time we become aware of the path of deepened intimacy with our self, others, the Sacred, and all of creation. Engaging the Spirit of the Heart is a lifelong venture that is undertaken with a companion, the Will of the Heart.

The Spirit of the Heart holds our intent to enter into authentic relationships. We do this through our desire to cause no harm. The Will of the Heart moves our intent into the arena of action. We move deeper into causing no harm by alleviating suffering. Very few people are so twisted in their own pain and suffering that they intentionally and willfully cause harm. Being hurtful or causing harm is typically the result of not being aware in the present moment. Our triggers latch on to us unaware. We lash out in reaction.

The Will of the Heart requires a cultivated state of awareness. This awareness permeates the internal and external worlds. Through full-body listening and compassionate response, we connect to our body/mind/spirit/heart, noticing what prevents us from being present. Perhaps we are worried about a child or have pulled a muscle. An impact in one aspect of our life throws us into the past or hurtles us into the future.

Our internal monologue is an ever-present source of distractions. Our intent is to be alert to our internal monologue and all other self-imposed distractions. Through this awareness, we discover how and where we are suffering. Armed with this knowledge, we take strides to alleviate that suffering. From this foundation, we help others release their anguish.

Integrating the Will of the Heart into our relationships requires that we know who we are. Within our authentic nature, we understand our limitations and accept our boundaries. I tend to be a fixer in relationships. When someone needs help, my instinct is through words and actions to change a situation to what I think is better. Unfortunately, my fixer desires often lead to compassion fatigue. Either my actions cannot improve a situation or I am left feeling undervalued. For me, accepting that I cannot fix another is a boundary that I am learning to keep in place. I am limited by my desire to fix. With this limitation, I cannot enter into intimate relationship.

When we are honest with our self about the need for boundaries and potential limitations, we are less likely to push past our capabilities in order to help another. Overextending our self in order to help another creates fragile connections. These connections are built upon illusions and an imbalance of power. Easily destroyed, they prevent us from creating a durable constellation of connections.

With accurate knowledge of our limitations and the pitfalls of our overextension, we gain a greater understanding of potential relationship constraints. We know which boundaries are hard and which ones can be nudged outward. When we shift our boundaries with courage and integrity, we open the self and the relationship to transformation.

The Will of the Heart invites us into a place of curious daring where we commit to being a healing presence. Healing begins first with our self. Old hurts and suffering are often deeply embedded and, at times, unrecognizable. We often ignore these constant companions or don't even realize that they exist. We may feel comforted by our hurts and suffering. We may feel we need them to survive. This is our illusion.

While we might survive in their presence, most assuredly we will not thrive. The Will of the Heart asks us to honestly identify our fears and perceived limitations. Identification of our festering wounds is the first step in healing our self and moving into a stronger, authentic connection with self, the Sacred, others, and all of creation.

The Will of the Heart recognizes that healing is a return to wholeness, not a restoration to the original form. This is the difference between healing our past hurts and resolving current suffering versus curing our suffering. We cannot return to the past or erase history. We can become a stronger, more durable, more authentic self by transmuting the suffering into catalysts of healing and transformation.

Buddhists believe we are never without suffering. We suffer and receive compassion, and suffering returns again. This is the cycle of our life. Through this life rhythm we become more authentic, courageous, and humble. Within this rhythm exists the potential for all of our relationships to deepen. We must enter the third aspect of this triad, the Feeling of the Heart, in order to live in intimate, authentic relationships.

The Spirit of the Heart is a reflection of our intent. The Will of the Heart manifests in our action. The Feeling of the Heart is where we live fully aware of the present moment. In this place we are aware of the positive and negative ramifications of our actions. In the Feeling of the Heart, we find opportunities to shift from a place of hurting and being stuck in an endless cycle of suffering to a place of healing and compassionate response.

Engaged compassion occurs on many levels and with full-body listening. It is both inward- and outward-focused. We experience compassion as living, dynamic, and flexible. Within the Feeling of the Heart lie possibilities. Through our awareness we perceive opportunities for compassionate action. Through this awareness we choose to respond or react. We either tightly close the eyes and ears of our heart in complacency or open them wide as we willingly transform into our highest, best self. This transformation positively impacts our contemplative relationship,

Therein lies the challenge. It is easy to be overwhelmed by all the distractions and reactions. These challenges can be overcome through hyperawareness. As we live in a state of hyper-noticing, we notice the bits and pieces of our life that we wish were different. The Feeling of the Heart requires that we accept life as it is, not as we wish it would be. Life, as it is, is filled with possibilities. These treasures are found in the present moment and are acted upon with curious daring.

Acceptance does not equal complacency. We are asked to look at our life and our relationships with the eyes of an objective observer. We notice how our triggers distract us. We don't expect to resolve all of life's triggers immediately. Rather, with awareness we choose what to release and what to celebrate as we move toward our true, best self.

Each authentic answer blows away more of the mist of illusion. We move deeply and with greater clarity into our authentic spirit. Acting upon our inner knowing helps us create a vibrant, compassionate life. Not living in complacency, we acknowledge and live out our possibilities. Within this vibrant energy we draw people to us. We create connections that are joy-filled. We live contemplatively in our constellation of connections.

Living from the Spirit, the Will, and the Feeling of the Heart requires courage and curious daring. If we see a possibility but are unable to respond to it, we may never connect fully with another. I met a woman at a meeting and was unsure of any points of deepening connection. With courage and curious daring, the tentative beginnings of relationship began. This relationship continues to deepen and expand.

By engaging all three aspects of the heart, we choose a different way. This way leads us deeply into our authentic essence. It provides the fuel to sustain the glowing ember of our divine spark. Each step along the trail of the heart requires courage and integrity. These renew our vigor. We discover how to live life to its fullest, which is a life fully in relationship.

Through relationship we sprinkle the sparks of joy, love, and compassion in each moment and in each person and in each part of creation with which we come in contact. This heart way of living radically shifts how we participate in relationship. Through the Spirit, the Will, and the Feeling of the Heart, our relationships transform into viable, loving, compassion-filled ones. Our constellation of connections is a thriving community of intimate relationships.

Creating a Constellation of Connections

Sit quietly. Focus on your breathing. Do not try to shift your breathing. Allow it to naturally flow in and out. Just notice. Individually focus on each of the three aspects of the heart using the following questions.

Spirit of the Heart: unspoken intent, desire to be in relationship

- Reflect upon a relationship. Using the 4nons (nonattachment, nonjudgment, nondefensiveness, nonviolence), describe how you react and respond to the other.
- What are your expectations of your partner and the relationship? How do these expectations impact your intent?
- Do you need to change your intent? If so, restate it.

Will of the Heart: awareness of our responses and reactions

- Return to the same relationship.
- Reflect upon several interactions with your partner that profoundly impacted the relationship.
- How did you react and respond in those situations?
- How did your intent manifest through your actions?
- How can your awareness empower you to live authentically through your intent?

Feeling of the Heart: connecting our intent to action with awareness

- Continue to use the same relationship during reflection.
- Either reset or reaffirm your intent to be in this relationship.
- Through courage and curious daring, create new ways of response that are in alignment with your intent.
- How does the implementation of this plan bring about relational transformation?

Chapter 10

The Guiding Presence of Relationship

Compassion radiates from the center of our being. It is shared first with our self. Without self-compassion it is impossible to effectively share compassion with another. Our experience of soothing our own woundedness creates the base from which we alleviate suffering in others. When we reach out to another in compassion-filled ways, we disrupt the status quo of a relationship. We realize compassion has no agenda or motive other than to be a balm for the spirit.

If engaging in compassion-filled ways is new to the relationship, an imbalance may become more pronounced. As the sharing of compassion realigns both partners, the relationship restructures and the level of trust increases. Deepened intimacy occurs. The power of compassion to transform our self, others, and relationships becomes apparent.

Compassion is never a manipulative force. Through compassion we look at the other with different eyes. We recognize the potential to grow and develop intimacy in each connection. Instead of being stuck, we easily flow within the dynamic, flexible relationship matrix. Within the matrix we sustain thriving relationships. With compassion we nurture these relationships.

Relationships are not static. Each, for better or worse, has its own ebb and flow. At times our connections are in sync while, in other moments, nothing we do will bring us into alignment with our partner. In those moments, instead of struggling, we enter into the ebb, move with the flow, and allow compassion to soothe the discord. We enter a place of greater understanding through intimacy created by respect and understanding.

Relationships are avenues through which we learn. Each compassionate act, whether from us or directed toward us, provides an opportunity for personal growth and evolution. Our response or reaction to compassion reveals much about our relationship with self. Falling into the same traps of reacting ingloriously to the same triggers provides clues to illusions under which we are laboring. Refusing to accept compassion leaves us chained to our illusions.

In order to evolve, we must reflect. Stopping, centering, and breathing compassion will bring us firmly into the ground of our being. These simple steps open the gate of our heart enough for us to accept compassion or to allow compassion to flow through us. We also tuck away the knowledge of our ability to receive or accept compassion for future reference.

The RI^2 process (reflection, introspection, and integration) is beneficial when discerning and attempting to remove the barriers that prevent us from accepting compassion. Here we engage our silence, and the noise of distractions in our quiet mind becomes clearer. When we hear with all of our senses, we better understand how the noise may direct our daily interactions in distracting ways. The sacred, intuitive voice of compassion nudges us back into alignment. We have only to listen. We reflect upon what we have heard, seek understanding during introspection, and integrate our knowing.

The alignment of our relationship with self is the catalyst to move into sync with our other relationships. No matter how beautiful, how loving, or how gentle a relationship with our self is, we will be unable to share the depth of connection unless we continually assess our relationship with self and make the revisions that draw us deeper into authenticity.

There is nothing magical about this shift from tumult to intuitive openness in any relationship. In fact, this evolution requires hard work, honesty, and humility. The evolution to ever-deepening, intimate relationships naturally occurs when we stop judging and blaming our self or others. Seeing life challenges as opportunities instead of disappointments makes us more receptive to contemplative relationships. We are honest about what prevents us from deeply engaging and humbly accepting our role in any difficulties.

Shifting from seeing disappointments to seeing opportunities occurs when we focus our attention on the awareness of the Sacred in every aspect of our life, including those perceived disappointments and challenges. We fully enter into awareness of the moment by acknowledging and then taming our inner critic. Compassion is a full-body, multisensory experience. In our moments of awareness, compassion becomes the grace-filled companion in our constellation of connections.

When our relationship with self is infused with compassion, we deeply and intentionally transform our other relationships through compassion. Recognizing our own triggers and distractions may inadvertently deepen old wounds and create new ones. With the balm of self-compassion, we gain the opportunity to forgive past transgressions and make peace with old hurts. Forgiving our self and others requires humility. Only when I humbly accept my embarrassing behaviors and intentionally shift my words and actions am I able to take steps on the road to profound and lasting change.

With humility we identify and accept our flaws, our humanness. We do this in ways that are freeing and do not debase us. Humbly we are able to see the potential for transformation through acceptance of our imperfections. When we shine the light of self-compassion on them, we discover the lesson in each experience. We shift our perception and understanding of these flaws and imperfections from suspicion and dislike to opportunities of grace.

We recognize our humanness, our perceived flaws, as the roots of our suffering. Suffering triggered by our thoughts, words, and actions is a constant companion guaranteed to help us practice humility and call upon self-compassion. Each moment of compassion and humility draws us more fully into intimate relationships. Self-acceptance leads to acceptance of others.

Adopting a stance of humility reveals the infinite possibilities that exist within each opportunity and gives us the courage and strength to view others differently. We look beyond perceived flaws and become more aware of pain and suffering in our self, others, and the world. With humility we draw closer to the other and invite a deeper connection. This connection is strengthened as we become aware of the compassion that flows from our heart, wraps around our entire being, and surrounds others. Compassion flows from the other back to us in a never-ending cycle of sharing.

With this renewed awareness of our self comes an awareness of our role in each of our relationships. We reflect on the nature of each relationship and how we contribute to it. Compassion enables us to ask and respond to the most difficult questions. What are our needs, hopes, and dreams of the relationship? Are they in alignment with those of our partner? How am I called to be in relationship?

As we discover the responses, we become aware of the need to alleviate suffering. It becomes as necessary as breathing. This energy provides the resources for us to discover a new peace. Securing a new, compassion-filled space may not be comfortable, but once it is obtained our relationships shift.

Relationships are dynamic and flexible. Each goes through the cycle of birth, growth, and release. Some relationships may never truly end but may go through this never-ending cycle. It isn't until we die that some relationships end. Others last a much shorter time. But none remain exactly the same over the course of the relationship's life. Compassion provides the glue of connectivity that helps us meet the other where they are, while being true to our self. In our truth we understand and accept the fluid nature of our constellation of connections.

During the life cycle of a relationship, the internal and external flows of compassion are vital. If we are not filled with self-compassion, we may turn our angst and judgments inward. We may feel alone in the relationship or feel that only we have the power to resolve any issues. We may be unaware of how much suffering this way of believing causes. The angst of this suffering may turn outward, and we then act in ways that hurt or harm others.

Life as it is becomes focused on our personal failure and perceived inabilities. Instead of being buoyed by compassion, we are mired in complacency caused by suffering. We cannot see past the shroud of suffering; the beauty of possibility is invisible. We are blind to the possibilities with which life graces us. We need a force that will impel us through the mist of illusion and into a space where we transform into our most authentic self.

Self-compassion calms the angst of our own suffering. We see the others in this vast planet not as adversaries but as fellow travelers. We realize the indisputable fact that we are all in this together. Each of us struggles to live to our highest potential. We all slip, fall, and skin our knees. Our role in each relationship is to acknowledge that life may be difficult and filled with suffering, to encourage our self and our partner to practice self-compassion, and to share compassion with others. Holding grudges or plotting revenge becomes impossible.

Compassion-centric relationships are both flexible and interdependent. When I was a youth worker in the 1990s, I won the Indiana Youth Investment Award. A beautiful wooden sculpture was part of the gift. This work of art consists of two beautifully flowing pieces of wood leaning toward one another yet not touching. It reflects interdependence, not codependence. My role in those relationships forged with youth was to compassionately journey with them as they learned who they were. I supported them while encouraging self-discovery and self-sufficiency. This compassionate way of journeying is the foundation of all relationships.

As I reflect upon that memory, I realize that interdependence is the potential grace found within each relationship. When we act upon the realization that we cannot function without connections, the power of contemplative relationship becomes evident. We create a web of interdependence while nurturing the divine spark of each individual. Spinning this intricate web and ensuring each strand's strength are only possible through compassion.

Within our quiet mind the spark of compassion flares. In the resulting light we see clearly the intricate web of connection and are able to navigate the rough patches of angry, pointing fingers and self-recrimination. Empowered by all forms of compassion, our connection to others strengthens. Our relationship is able to withstand crisis.

When all involved in relationship willingly practice compassion, the relationship as a whole and partners as individuals transform into their most authentic selves. This transformation is not a one-time occurrence. Contemplative relationships invite us to discover again and again our most authentic self. Compassion and this ongoing discovery of the authentic might not be easy, but it is rewarding.

Authenticity cannot be faked. For brief moments we may be able to spin an illusion of who we are, and we, and others, may accept this as truth. When we are aware of relationship dynamics, we are better able to identify what is superficial and illusory. We gain a greater understanding of our partner's interactions with us. With trust and humility we share our realizations and banish the illusions, thus moving beyond superficial connections.

Authentic compassion cannot be faked. While certain aspects of compassion may feel like pity or empathy, the depth and breadth of the grace of compassion are more than those two emotions. The goal of compassion is to alleviate suffering. It manifests in so many different ways, but the end result is the same: the alleviation of suffering. With wide openness, without judgment, and through unconditional love, compassion manifests. We learn how to move our self and the relationship into greater intimacy. When compassion imbues us, we become a radical transformer.

Creating a Constellation of Connections

Sit quietly. Focus on your breathing. Do not try to shift your breathing. Allow it to naturally flow in and out. Through your breath, enter the ground of your being. See the beautiful garden that you have planted and nurtured. Name those parts of your self that are not authentic—the parts of you that are wounded and prevent you from being your true self.

After naming and being with those "imperfections," call upon the wisdom of your self-compassion. Soothe the suffering. This soothing is the bedrock of our self-compassion. Ask yourself what is the most loving, compassionate response to me? The answer may be through verbal affirmation, exercise, or some other self-directed kindness. Whatever the answer, the goal is to alleviate your suffering.

As self-compassion fills your being, visualize the well spilling over and touching others.

How does your compassion deepen your relationship with self?

How does self-compassion invite you into greater authenticity?

How does self-compassion increase your ability to share compassion with others?

In what ways has the intimacy in your relationships with others deepened through compassionate action?

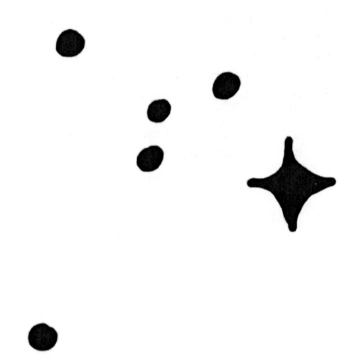

Stars = Divine sparks of compassion

Chapter 11

The Radical Transformer

We live fully integrated in our constellation of connections. Each of our relationships provides clues to our relationship with our self. Within each of these connections lies our challenges and our greatest opportunities for learning and growth. We are able to meet those challenges only when we drink from the well of compassion found deep within our divine spark.

The power to radically transform resides both in our self and also in all those with whom we connect through relationship. Compassion is an transformational guide. As we share compassion with our self and others, it lights our authentic self and casts shadows on the falsehoods of our illusions. While compassion may not always be present in ways we want, this spark of the Sacred brings us to our most authentic, honest being.

Our actions, when guided by our spark of compassion, are never counterfeit. When we align our spirit with compassion, our courage bubbles to the surface. We may recognize our fear and uncertainty, but our need to be a font of compassion moves us through this fear to mercy. What begins as mercy emanating from the source of the Sacred is imprinted into our spirit in the form of patience and love. With mercy, patience, and love we meet others authentically and encourage them to find that place within.

Each time we choose compassion, we create paths of awareness. The world morphs into an extraordinary place filled with possibilities. The way we engage others is supercharged by our conscious intent; the options for navigating our constellation of connections multiply. Through this new way of seeing the world, we forge new types of connections. Within the silence, we share our compassion in ever-deepening communion.

This is a multifaceted awareness in which we intimately recognize the suffering of our self and others. Eyes open, we see when and how we cause harm. It is not that it becomes easier to cause no harm; rather, we become aware of our potential to cause harm. With this awareness we choose to respond instead of react. And, through our response, we strive to alleviate any suffering.

Through compassionate action, we shift into a place of possibility. No longer are we bound by illusion. We know that the lessening of suffering is possible through us. This inner knowing fuels our creative expression of compassion. We search for ways to reframe our life and creatively soothe suffering hearts. In these moments we discover a greater intimacy with our self and others.

Our intent to be compassionate, coupled with our action, begins a spiral of healing energy. An authentic, compassionate act doesn't stop at the intended recipient. It spirals forth, touching others in profound, unexpected, transforming ways. Our intended recipient may either unconsciously or intentionally share compassion. Compassion ultimately flows to where it is needed.

Through the alleviation of suffering, compassion is paid forward in minute and grandiose ways. The very act of compassion has the potential to shift both our awareness in and our perception of life. We may choose to live as a bodhisattva by vowing to alleviate suffering whenever possible and however possible. A bodhisattva, while not perfect in compassionate response, has taken a vow to alleviate suffering in the world.

When our intent is to be a sharer of compassion, we scatter the seeds of potential transformation. These seeds take root in places we never would have realized or consciously intended. We connect through relationship in unimaginable, profound ways. Through these connections, we encourage others to sow compassion and reap the resulting abundance in their lives.

Sharing compassion in a relationship creates pathways of deepened connections. This doesn't mean that practicing compassion is easy. Even when we want to share compassion, our pathway to action may be fraught with obstacles, including self-doubts. We may fear that our compassion may be misconstrued or refused. We may fear that another may view it as pity or something other than compassion. Acting to alleviate suffering calls us into courageous presence.

The way of the bodhisattva is not for the faint-hearted. Being a font of compassion, an alleviator of suffering, requires courage and a willingness to rely upon our intuition. We must live in awareness of our self and our motives and assumptions. Compassion invites us into an ever-deepening understanding of self. We recognize that compassion flowing from our authentic self carries within its courageous heart the potential for radical, sustained transformation.

Radical transformation requires that we move outside our comfort zone and don the cape of courage. This is not a cape of a superhero; rather, this is the persona of one who sees beyond the mundane and ordinary to see and peer deeply into the extraordinary world. We acknowledge those people and things we hold in deep reverence while celebrating the sacred inherent in all. Living in this world, the radical transformer helps others perceive the extraordinary in their lives. While we are not a superhero, we become a compassion hero.

Courage is strengthened with humility. We admit that while we do not have the answers to eradicate all suffering, we do have the grace to create the environment where compassion flourishes and suffering is alleviated. This environment is the result of being in harmony with self and others. When in harmony, we seek to understand differences and are respectful even when we do not agree. This balance is gained through humbly resting in the silence of our quiet mind.

While we may not have the answers, humility invites us to reach out to others and offer our gifts. We discern within our quiet mind which gifts to share. By attending to our verbal and nonverbal internal monologue, we acknowledge and release our arrogant tendencies. Then our compassionate responses to our intuitive nudges become greater than our desire to react from our fears. Each time we choose to respond instead of react, our relationships grow in their contemplative nature. We are aware of the interconnectivity of life as we more firmly connect to the triad of our self, the Sacred, and the other.

Relationships thrive when rooted in the ground of our being. Unless they are rooted in this place of love, any relationship will wither. The ground of our being is accessed through silence, where we nurture and grow each relationship. Within the silence, our compassion sparks the compassion of another. In that flash, a connection is created. We spend the lifetime of the relationship nurturing this connection while being aware of its organic, fragile nature.

Relationships are flexible and organic. They are also fragile. Sometimes we may take another person or the relationship for granted. The relationship may become brittle. We may believe that we know best, and our humility may flee. We may struggle with being compassionate or feel the other is not deserving of our compassion. Unless we are honest, authentic, and courageous, the relationship may self-destruct.

Even if we feel that our stream of compassion is dammed or feel that our compassion has dried up, the end of the relationship is not necessarily a given. Now is the time to reflect upon the connection and discern if the relationship is still viable in its current form. When we realize a relationship must change, we discern how to accomplish the shift in a life-giving way.

Through the 4nons—nonattachment, nonjudgment, nondefensiveness, and nonviolence—we discover ways to infuse compassion into our self and the other in order to transform the relationship. The 4nons pave the pathway of the objective observer. With this stance, we recognize that the health of the relationship is possible only when both partners are actively engaged.

During this reflection time, we flood our self with compassion. We first acknowledge how we suffer, and then we search for the roots of suffering. Next, we release suffering that comes from clinging too tightly to what we want. We name any illusory perceptions of the relationship. Compassion asks us to loosen the tight grip we have on illusions. Only when we are nonattached to our desires and illusions can we open our self to living authentically in the relationship. The relationship is no longer caught in a stranglehold of want, so it can breathe into a new way of being.

Through nonattachment, we identify our judgments and begin the courageous task of identifying the fear-filled roots of our reactions. We accept our role in the disintegration of any relationship while refusing to defend our reactions. We pay particular attention to the violence birthed through our thoughts, words, and actions. Through nonattachment, we are better able to know our judgments but not cause harm by acting upon them. In the same way, we know when we have erred. Instead of defending our behavior, we change it. Through relationship, we learn how to be a truer, better self.

This stance opens us to receiving self-compassion. Accepting that we are attached, judgmental, defensive, and violent rips away our illusions and bruises our authentic self. With this bruising comes opportunities for healing and transformation. We heal by acknowledging how our illusions have prevented us from living authentically and by forgiving our self. Transformation occurs when we reframe our life by releasing the illusions and accepting the beauty and grace within us.

Self-compassion alleviates our suffering and moves us into a place where we accept our flaws so that we may transform into a more authentic being. Compassion directed toward the self also heals the cracks in our authentic being. When we open our hearts, the Spirit, the Will, and the Feeling of the Heart naturally integrate into our everyday life.

Through our compassionate commitment, we keep our hearts open and receptive while in relationship. Even with this commitment, our triggers may flip and our heart may shut down. We react. In those moments, awareness is the key. Through awareness we find ways to keep open the gateway of the heart. Our reactions shift to responses and we minimize the unintentional harm we cause in our relationships. Keeping the gate open and compassion flowing occurs through the acknowledgment of our triggers and being diligently aware of situations that exacerbate our reactions. Transformation doesn't happen at once. We transform minute by minute through a radical stance of curious daring.

Each of us has certain phrases, situations, and people that are guaranteed to trigger reactions. These potential catalysts are terrific practice arenas. After reacting, we can dissect what happened to discover not only what stimulated the trigger but also why the catalyst threw us off-kilter. Seldom does the actual host of the catalyst have anything to do with the reaction. Like a light switch flipped, the trigger illuminates deep-seated fears, anxieties, and feelings of scarcity. Moving beyond these barriers is possible only through courageous action.

As part of an all-volunteer committee, I found myself becoming frustrated with one member. While he had great ideas, he never seemed to put them into action. He also liked to connect me to others in ways that were not helpful. Each time he would share an idea or another connection, I found myself tensing and reacting.

Using RI² (reflection, introspection, and integration), I sought to discover the roots of my reactions. I recognized that I am a pleaser and fixer. I felt guilty about saying no or not following through with his suggestions. (This has been one of my lifelong patterns.) So, with great difficulty, I began to shift this pattern. As I listened to him, I listened to my internal monologue. Through bi-listening, I was able to thank him while affirming my right to choose how to follow up on the suggestions. While we may not be the best of friends, we are no longer adversaries.

When I discover what lies at the core of my reaction, I flood myself and others with compassion. With this flow of compassion comes the power to heal my woundedness. My awareness invites me into greater understanding of how I am being triggered and increases the potential of developing a response that replaces the reactions. Each time I respond instead of react, I fortify a pattern of response and minimize the chance of reaction. The cycle of reaction is broken. We move into a different way of connection through building more compassionate pathways of response.

Moving into compassionate response happens with an engaged heart. Through the Spirit of the Heart we affirm our commitment to creating a world free of harm. The Will of the Heart desires active participation in alleviating suffering. With this commitment we agree to be vessels of compassion. Finally, through the Feeling of the Heart we enter into a deeply compassionate life. We become radical transformers and compassion warriors. We toss out our complacent attitude and live life with courage and curious daring. We dive deeper into the well of compassion to grasp intimacy with our self and others. This intimacy is possible through a full-body, all-encompassing form of communicating: communion.

Creating a Constellation of Connections

Sit quietly. Focus on your breathing. Do not try to shift your breathing. Allow it to naturally flow in and out. Through your breath, enter the ground of your being. Visualize the garden you have sown, nurtured, and harvested in your self.

- What parts of the garden are authentic?
- What is growing your illusions?
- Reflect upon a particular relationship.
- How do you authentically share with the other?
- In what ways are you humble?
- Where have you been courageous?
- How could engaging your humility, courage, and authenticity strengthen this relationship?

Chapter 12

Full-Body Communication

Within our mind we conceive our thoughts, words, and actions. By cultivating a quiet mind, we are able to listen to how the internal monologue generates our thoughts, words, and actions. In the inky night sky of our silence, our thoughts, words, and actions are more likely to be conceived without the interference of our distractions. Minimizing distractions enables us to live in compassionate response.

Through cultivation of our quiet, silence is always with us. We can choose to return to the silence at any moment of any day. Even when we are overwhelmed by life's tumult, the comfort of silence is available to us when we focus our awareness on the present moment. The warm embrace of silence whispers, "I am here. Lean on me. In me find the way through distractions."

Although with practice it becomes easier to access silence, a great chasm exists within our self. We cross this chasm through connections forged in relationships with the self, the Sacred, others, and all of creation. As we rest in the great inkiness of the night sky, our divine spark of compassion yearns to bridge the chasm and discover the grace of deep intimate connection. We build this bridge of sustainable connection through communion.

What is this thing we call communion? Thomas Merton's description is one of my favorites: "It is wordless. It is beyond words, and it is beyond speech, and it is beyond concept."[10] For me, communion is this and more. It is a blend of words and no words, a way to engage full-body listening and compassionate response.

Communion is an experience of engagement through all of our senses. We enter into a state of hyperawareness in which we transcend the mundane and move into the extraordinary. Within this space, relationships evolve into greater intimacy.

In the tumult and busyness of our days, we have just forgotten this way of being connected. We can learn to access this way of communicating through full-body listening. We bi-listen, focusing on our responses and reactions while listening intently to another. Through communion we create intimacy in relationship. Resting in the inky darkness of silence while nurturing our spark of compassion, we respond to others by using communion. We are aware of each potential connection and are compelled to connect. We are intentionally present and gloriously awake to the extraordinary created through connection with the other. With words and without, we recognize and celebrate the sparks of compassion in one another.

The earliest experience of communion that I remember occurred when I was a young child during the celebration of the Eucharistic liturgy in a Catholic church. As I chanted in Latin with the priest and then responded with the congregation, the Sacred connected me to the community in the church, creating a mystical experience. I can still feel, with all my senses, the extraordinary nature of that moment. I did not know where I ended and where the community began. My divine spark flared, and I felt the responding glow of the embers of others. I was connected without words to the community of worship and to the Sacred. We spoke to one another with our entire beings.

As I grew older my understanding of communion deepened. Both by accident and through intent, I discovered that communion could be experienced in places other than communal worship. Communion was present wherever an environment of silence existed. All I needed to do was infuse my spirit with compassion and allow the tendrils to reach out to others. I could experience communion in every moment of every day by focusing my attention on the awareness of the Sacred in myself, each person, and all of creation. This realization shifted my relationships from mundane to contemplative.

Communion has become the preferred way for me to communicate. Only when I am in the moment and aware am I able to enter into this full-body way of dialoguing. If I am distracted, I miss opportunities to really know the other. Distractions inhibit the ability to engage full-body listening and compassionate response. The connectors that join our divine spark are unable to fully develop and strengthen unless we perceive the world through all of our functioning senses.

We are multisensory beings who live in four realms: the physical, mental, emotional, and spiritual These four aspects of self are at the core of our divine spark. When they act in tandem, our awareness is increased. We are better able to sift through the constant bombardment of information. Strengthening our ability to gain information in each aspect and through each sense increases our ability to respond with communion.

Like the practice of compassion, communion requires that we move from our heads and our analytical, logical mind to communicate with our heart. Intuitively, what begins in the heart radiates outward to encompass our body, mind, and spirit. It is not that the other aspects of our being are less important; rather, beginning with our heart creates a different pathway to living through experience.

Beginning in the heart, we are more in touch with our feelings. In this place, we are more likely to create an environment in which we move beyond the mundane and experience the extraordinary. Through the connection of heart, body, mind, and spirit we become a fully integrated being who reaches out and shares intimately with others. This intimate connection is forged through communion.

When we step through the gateway of communion, our relationships gain greater intimacy. We share on a deeper level, and our level of trust increases. The pathway to intimacy is paved with communion. Intimacy happens when we look in the eyes of another and connect by recognizing their spirit. When we are in this place we are no longer bound by perceived divisions. We see the older unity that Merton speaks of when he reminds us: "My dear brothers, we are already one. But we imagine that we are not. And what we have to recover is our original unity."[11]

The three aspects of our constellation of connections are not separate nor is one more important than the others. We may feel a certain kinship with one aspect or have difficulty engaging another. We do not have to attain perfection in using the three aspects for them to be effective. Through silence, compassion, and communion, we continue to seek ways to deepen our understanding of how each aspect impacts each relationship and our constellation as a whole. Using this understanding, we act in ways that bring personal and relationship transformation.

When we intentionally create our night sky through our interactions with self, others, the Sacred, and all of creation, we increase our contemplative traits. We do not experience the contemplative life of a monk. As a contemplative, we live fully in the life we have. The physical, mental, emotional, and spiritual aspects integrate into one. Each moment becomes an opportunity to acknowledge and incorporate into our life the many ways that the Sacred manifests to us.

Scheduling regular moments to rest in the silence creates a healthy rhythm for our lives. As silence becomes a comforting and comfortable space, we more easily enter our quiet mind. We hear and respond to our internal monologue while avoiding reacting to our distractions. In each moment of response, we rekindle the ember of our divine spark. Compassion flows to us, through us, and beyond us. As compassion flows from us into the world, the invisible connectors of communion flare. When we engage others, their compassion flows to us. Communion happens.

Communion is a flaring of compassion across invisible connectors. Compassion sparks off the connectors of communion and impacts others. Creating a domino effect, each compassion action impacts still others. In this way we create and sustain our constellation of connections. We rest in the silence that feeds the compassion of our divine spark, which nurtures our ability to enter into communion, which expands the silence in our quiet mind. And the infinite possibility of contemplative relationship is revealed.

When we enter into communion, our attention is focused on the present moment. If we are backward-focused on past regrets and guilt or forward-focused on worries and hopes, our awareness is drawn away from what is happening in the moment. We miss the minute cues that could guide our response. We react. Our fragile relationships become brittle and may collapse. Our reactions minimize our ability to enter deeply into the connection of unity. Communion invites us to shift from a cycle of reactivity to one where our intent manifests in compassionate response. Each response moves us into a greater connection. In this place of unity, we recognize that everything is relationship.

Living in deep awareness of the importance of communion offers us a choice. We can choose to be superficial in our connections, just skimming the surface of the other, and miss opportunities to live extraordinarily. Or we can commit to living in communion. In deep communication, we fully engage and discover who and what lie at the core of being. Peering deeply into this core and responding with compassion to what we find there engages our many life connections. We are aware of the extraordinary in more intimate ways.

Through communion we enter the land of common ground. In this arena we cast aside judgments and the obsessive need to be right at all costs. Our focus is to understand and to garner mutual respect. While we may not fully agree with the other, communion requires an attitude of reverence toward all. When we reach this place of understanding through reverence, the tumult in our life lessens. Through the connectors of communion we move into a peace-filled place.

Developing and maintaining a practice of communion takes time, energy, and diligence. We agree to be authentic while clarifying our role and responsibilities in maintaining our connections. Without courage and humility, we could not maintain the open-mindedness that is a precursor to understanding our relationships with our authentic self, the Sacred, others, and all of creation.

Communion reveals a world of limitless possibilities of connection. In this arena, we can enthusiastically connect in creative, flexible, and dynamic ways. In doing this, we continuously create the space where communion not only thrives but is inevitable. This deep form of communication begins and ends with our relationship to our self. Connecting with others is dependent upon the strength and health of our connection to self.

Creating a Constellation of Connections

Sit quietly. Focus on your breathing. Do not try to shift your breathing. Allow it to naturally flow in and out. Through your breath, enter the ground of your being. With awareness engage your full-body listening as a way of entering into communion. Before beginning a conversation take a moment of self reflection.

Close your eyes. Take a couple of breaths. Allow yourself to enter into the present moment. Be aware of your distractions. Name them and release them. Engage in full-body listening by through the following:

Take a couple of breaths while listening to and feeling the rhythm of your breath. How is the cadence of your breath affecting your ability to connect fully and intentionally?

Take a couple of breaths and notice any physical sensations. Is there tension in your body? Tingling? What do you feel? How are the sensations affecting your ability to connect fully and intentionally?

Take a couple of breaths and deeply inhale the world around you. What do you smell? How is this sensation affecting your ability to connect fully and intentionally?

Take a couple of breaths and notice what your mouth tastes like. How is this sensation affecting your ability to connect fully and intentionally?

Now, intentionally affirm your desire to release any distractions. Take another couple of breaths. Fully enter into a conversation or a personal reflection.

How was your awareness different? How did you respond?

Chapter 13

A Contemplative Spirit

When communion permeates the nooks and crannies of our silence, we see through new eyes. Our seeing becomes a full-body experience that incorporates all of our senses. We hear the phrase "it isn't all about you" and realize that life really is all about us and our choice of reaction or response to every moment, every situation, every person, and every thing. Being in communion with another requires that we are impeccable in our words and authentic in our actions.

Communion is a heart-to-heart connection. While I cannot force another to communicate with communion, the way that I relate may coax them into this place of deep communication. Communion always occurs in a safe place that is built and fortified when we are aware, authentic, courageous, humble, clear-seeing, enthusiastic, and open-minded. By modeling these seven aspects of a contemplative spirit, our life becomes a fertile place where communion occurs naturally and spontaneously. We become one with others.

Awareness

When we are aware in the present moment, we are fully alive. Unaware, we are more easily lured into the between place—between our regrets and sorrows of the past and our hopes and fears of the future. But we have the power of choice. We choose when we are present.

Often the choice not to be present is made unconsciously when we are overwhelmed by past memories or swept headlong into the dreams of the future. Stuck in this place of worry, angst, and hope, we lose the choice of being present. Being aware requires cultivating an environment of silence. Within this silence, we recognize the power of distraction to firmly root us in the past or the future. Within the silence, we are aware of opportunities to respond with generosity and compassion.

With this awareness, we peer beyond the common and mundane. Resting in the extraordinary increases our awareness of the pitfalls of reacting. Even in split-second decisions, compassion helps us to both bypass our impulses to react and glimpse into the extraordinary as we take strides into different ways of responding in relationship. The extraordinary is a place of possibility. Navigating relationships contemplatively becomes the norm when we are in this place of deep reverence.

Through our constellation of connections, we create new relationships and strengthen old ones. Within relationship we respond to opportunities to be compassionate, share joy, and live with poignancy, crafted by curious daring and courage. We are aware of our choice to be authentic or to engage in superficial relationships. Across the inky darkness of silence, we share our compassionate presence and enter into communion.

Awareness is a state of high noticing. Our interactions are no longer about reactions to the words or facial expressions of another. We begin to acknowledge intuitive nudges that guide us to respond in loving, gentle ways. We are fully awake to the compassion that flows to, in, and through us, and with awareness we reach a new level of being. Our responses are the results of deep connection. Communion happens as a result of our authentic, honest core.

Authenticity

We may find it is easy to hide behind the mask of a person we think others want to see and know. When we put on that public face, we risk becoming deeply entrenched in the illusion of who others think we are. We may believe this public face is who we are until the illusions becomes so tangled with our authentic self that separating our true self from the illusions may be almost impossible. The way to unravel the tangle of illusion is through reflection, discernment, and communion.

Being authentic requires ongoing reflection and honest discernment accomplished during moments of communion. Discovering the reasons why we react and respond is neither a simple nor an easy process. We may fear the changes required by the answers or believe that our true self is not enough to share. Until we identify what lies at the ground of our being and embrace our authentic nature, any connection we have with another will be diluted by illusion. Our authentic self is the light that guides others not only to authentic relationship but also to their authentic nature. Communion is possible through a triad of authenticity—self, other, relationship.

By accepting our authentic being, we acknowledge who we are—the good and the perceived shadow. As we take steps to let go of misrepresentations, we agree to live in awareness. We understand the necessity of sharing our true nature.

Acting in ways that mirror our authentic nature is the initial step to embracing our authenticity . Being aware of how our actions mirror what is authentic and what is illusion guides us in choosing how we respond. Through reflection and discernment, we discover additional steps that draw us closer to our true self. Becoming our authentic self is a scary proposition. It means not only acknowledging what is false but also eliminating it from our life. Being fully authentic requires courage.

Courage

The Cowardly Lion in The Wizard of Oz is an appropriate persona to illustrate the time-old battle between courage and fear. He was so in touch with the plethora of fears, uncertainties, and angst in his life that he believed the illusion that he was nothing more than his fears. He could not identify his actions as courageous.

In truth, awareness of his fears provided the tools to awaken his courage. Courage became the weapon of victory.

Instead of allowing his fears to overwhelm him, the Cowardly Lion honestly acknowledged them. Through his acknowledgement of fear, he became aware of his choices. He made courageous choices fully cognizant of his fears. His fears did not stop him from living; rather, fear impelled him to never give in to his uncertainties. Curious daring became the impetus for his life.

Like the Cowardly Lion, we don't suddenly wake up one morning to find that all of our fears have disappeared. Instead, we wake up to an awareness of our fears. We acknowledge them and recognize their potential impact on our lives. With RI2 (reflection, introspection, and integration), we dig deeply into the ground of our being to discover the fears at the root of each illusion. No longer do they have a chokehold on our actions. With awareness we choose to dissolve the fear-generated barriers to living authentically.

Each time we name a fear, we are given a choice. Even if we cannot completely banish fear from our life, we can take strides to minimize its impact. Being authentic does not come from a lack of fears; being authentic requires their recognition and not allowing the resulting illusions to paralyze us. Being courageous is not always a grand gesture. It is a quiet, unassuming way of being. When we are authentic, we hold courage in one hand and humility in the other.

Humility

Humility requires a gentle, unpretentious stance of awareness. When we are humble, we know who we are in our deep authentic core without the need to broadcast that information. We have a clear understanding of our strengths and weaknesses. We are aware of our capabilities, talents, and skills. We share them in courageous, loving ways. We understand that our gifts do not make us better; rather, they prepare us to be partners in contemplative relationship.

Humility demands that we place no requirements or conditions on our relationships. We are fully aware of our expectations, but we limit their impact. When a relationship needs to transition, we are able to acknowledge, without judgment, the need for change and then initiate the shift. A humble heart recognizes there is no blame; there are only opportunities for growth.

With humility comes a certain comfort in our authentic nature. When we are comfortable in who we are, the path to our divine spark is brightly lit. We express our self through compassion. With compassion we easily separate what is true and authentic from the false, illusory faces we often project out of fear.

Without courage, what we believe to be humility may in fact be low self-image or a lack of self-value. Our connections and communication with others will lack depth. While we may understand the possibility of communion, realizing this state of connection may be difficult, if not impossible. Until we can accept our greatness with humility, we will not find the gateway of communion.

Courage and humility are intricately woven together. When we combine the two, we create the space for communion. We open our self to the other in ways that encourage understanding. Our humble spirit has no hidden agendas or motivations. Through humility, we expose our authentic nature. Sharing who we are at the core requires the realization that we may not be accepted. We have the strength and courage to rest in that knowledge. Humility and courage give us the clarity to acknowledge not only who we are but also the authentic nature of others.

Clarity

For many years Dewitt Jones was a National Geographic photographer. Over the course of those years, he discovered how to shift his perception from the mundane to the extraordinary. He shares this perception shift in a series of videos that focus on what is right with the world. Dewitt Jones believes that we can all learn to see the extraordinary in the world. This way of seeing happens in moments of clarity.

Clarity requires digging beneath the surface of the mundane to discover the sparkling gems of the extraordinary. With clarity, our perception shifts. We see beyond the surface and gain the ability to reframe the world into what is real from a contemplative stance. Instead of seeing what we believe is there, we see the potential of what truly exists.

The way past illusion is lit by our awareness of potential and possibility. Awareness requires that we open our eyes and ask what we are seeing. What we discover in clarity powers our voice. We articulate questions that bring greater understanding of the nature of each relationship. Through clarity we accept the privilege and responsibility inherent in relationship.

Relationships are no longer taken for granted. We understand how privileged we are to be invited into relationship. We recognize how privileged we are to be offered the opportunities to learn our life challenges. We appreciate the responsibility we have in learning our life lessons as well as in helping others learn theirs.

When we see clearly, the scales of illusion fall from our eyes. We cast aside our illusions and journey the path of authentic connection. We are fully aware that we do not lay the course; rather, with clarity we navigate the course with communion. We recognize that communion with our self and others nurtures both our humility and our courage. Humility and courage create the space for communion to occur. This journey to connection through communion is possible through the enthusiasm gained by curious daring.

Enthusiasm

At times we peer deeply into the reflection of who we are and choose to go through the motions of existing with our illusions as our closest companions. Being connected in superficial ways may seem comforting and easy. This way of encounter may be enough to sustain us in a place of half-life. This mere existence is not truly living. We are caught in a space of complacency. The way out of this complacency is through curious daring.

In this cloudy place of being, we do not fully connect to our true self or to anyone else. By calling upon our courage, we are able to question why we are content to live in this place of complacent existence. With curious daring we live from that answer. Curious daring encourages risk-taking; enthusiasm propels us toward radical transformation. In this transformation we find a different, more satisfying relationship model.

Any difficulties in relationships are reframed as opportunities for growth. We discover new ways to transform individuals and relationships. We reach our highest potential. Enthusiasm for a relationship does not mean we are stuck. Enthusiasm when paired with courage may provide the energy to move us into a different experience of relationship.

When we are enthusiastic, we live boldly. Curiously and energetically we delve into the ordinary while sure that the extraordinary is waiting to be discovered. We share who we are as invitation to greater intimacy. And our enthusiasm and curious daring nudge our partners to share their gifts with us. No longer mundane, life reveals itself as a miracle to recognize and embrace in each unfolding moment. Enthusiasm and curious daring thrive within an open mind.

Open-Mindedness

Life is expansive and filled with a myriad of opportunities. When we allow our preconceived notions and judgments to direct us, we live the illusion that walking a narrow path is the only way. Open-mindedness broadens our worldview. With courage we begin to challenge our self-constructed reality. Humbly, we admit what is false. With clarity we discover what is real. We search, knowing that even if our understanding is obscured by misconceptions, an open mind creates the fertile ground of true and honest knowing.

Being open-minded means adopting an attitude of "I am open to what I need to see." We acknowledge we may not have the right answers or even any answers. In our openness, we recognize that, through diligent awareness, the knowing will surface. Living life aware, with enthusiasm and curious daring, creates the space where, through communion, we discover the answers to our musings.

Open-mindedness invites us into the dynamic, flexible nature of relationship. Agenda gone, we can move within the flow while intuitively and compassionately responding to the other. Judgments are recognized; we avoid reacting by responding with compassion. We live in communion with others. This communion calls us to enter into a community of all.

Every day and in each moment of our life we connect through relationship. When we accept our true self, illusions lose their power. Without the tangle of illusions, we open our eyes and are aware of our authentic nature. Our true self responds with awareness. We rest in the comfort that comes from living a life based upon courage and humility. We are open to relationship shifts as we grow closer or grow apart from the partner.

As we respond from our awareness of the external world, we gain clarity about both the illusions and the authentic nature of others. With this knowledge we respond through our humble spirit, no matter what the distraction. Through all of this we are enthusiastically open-minded. With curious daring we take advantage of each opportunity to connect. We enter into and live in the potential and the reality of relationship through communion.

Creating a Constellation of Connections

Sit quietly. Focus on your breathing. Do not try to shift your breathing. Allow it to naturally flow in and out. Through your breath, enter the ground of your being. Enter into the awareness. Reflect upon how each attribute of self enhances your abilities to create and maintain communion.

Awareness
When your attention is in the moment, how do you respond? How are you able to prevent reactions?

Authenticity
How do your illusions prevent you from responding authentically?
How does the truth at the core of your being help identify and release illusions?

Courage
Name the fears that prevent you from speaking with honesty and integrity.
Call upon your courage to fashion a compassionate response to your self.

Humility
Notice how your judgments and arrogance drive your interactions.
How might you identify the barriers to connecting to an other with your humble heart?

Clarity
What fears, arrogance, or other illusions cloud the way that you perceive?
How can your awareness increase your clarity?

Enthusiasm
Reflect upon the barriers that prevent you from enthusiastically engaging another.
How might compassion to self and to others boost your enthusiastic spirit?

Open-Mindedness
What judgments, assumptions, and other illusions close your welcoming heart?
How might you use the first six traits to open your self?

Practice integrating one of these traits into your interactions. What shifts?

Chapter 14

Communion At the Core

Being contemplative increases our awareness of the importance of relationship. We understand with our entire being that everything in our life happens as a result of relationship. Without an authentic relationship with the self, we are unable to enter into deep, meaningful connection with others. With communion we move beyond our superficial façade and our illusions to connect deeply with our authentic self. Communion breathes life into the core of our being.

Communion enhances the environment of silence, and we move deeper into personal reflection and introspection. We listen to our internal monologue and respond to it genuinely and compassionately. We celebrate our strengths and identify our perceived weaknesses. During these moments of reflection, we rest in our heart space. We take steps to connect our heart with our head.

While in our heart space, we actively engage the 4nons: nonattachment, nonjudgment, nondefensiveness, and nonviolence. Using the 4nons, we become objective observers seeking to understand the depths of our woundedness. This understanding provides the conduit that connects us to the well of our compassion. The conduit of understanding reaches out. Through subsequent healing and our understanding of the power of connection, we reach out, sharing compassion with others.

Reflection requires that we search to understand how our life experiences impact us mentally, emotionally, spiritually, and physically. When in communion with our self, we do not attempt to fix or change anything. We understand and open our self to healing. Communion reveals a profound connection with the Source and with our self. Through these connections transformation occurs.

What begins with superficial aspects of interactions and our reactions and responses to them morphs into a vibrant relationship through communion. We dive beneath the surface to discover why some people and situations bring peace and why others trigger tumult, anger, and aggravation. Using the 4nons, we observe how we are perpetrators of peace and/or tumult. As an objective observer, we are unable to cling to our assumptions about what precipitated our reaction; we do not judge or defend our behavior. Our stance is nonviolent as we seek to understand and reach common ground.

It has been said that the greatest distance in the world is between our heart and our head. Often we find our emotions and our logical mind at odds. Through RI^2 we connect the heart with the head by practicing reflection and introspection. When we enter into introspection, we use the rich trove of information gained during reflection by our objective observer. We sort through the information and search for patterns of reaction and response.

Motives, judgments, and assumptions are revealed as we gain a clearer understanding of how we get caught by our triggers. We notice how and when we have violated the 4nons. Introspection is not self-castigation; rather, it leads us to greater understanding of our self and our interactions. It provides the clues to transformation of our self and our relationships. Introspection invites us to enter into communion with the self and to call upon self-compassion to be a balm for our suffering.

Without integration, reflection and introspection become an endless cycle of learning without the potential of resolution. Through integration we create strategies to potentially and successfully repattern a reaction into a response. This repatterning impacts first our relationship with self. As we rescript our lives, we acknowledge that we need not live in the mists of illusion. Each possible integration scenario has the seeds of living from the core of our being. Only through the birth of our true self do we ensure that we enter into and sustain intimate connection.

When we attend to relationships with RI2, we integrate a new way of being into our life. This new way of living includes communion with our self and others. Resting in the silence, we engage in communion by listening with our entire being. Full-body listening provides clues about our next steps. Communion with our self opens us to entering into communion with others. We are open to who and what journeys with us.

The journey with communion encompasses the relationship with our self. This is our primary relationship. If we are unable to engage communion at the core of our being, we will be blind and unable to comprehend the many tangible and intangible obstacles that litter the path of communion with the Sacred, others, and all of creation. We need not be in constant communion with our self in order to practice communion with others. As long as we engage in regular communion with our self, communion flourishes in other areas of our life.

Communion is not automatically present in our interactions. Deep communion in relationship does not deepen by following a logical step-by-step process, and we do not gain the ability to enter into communion through self-practice alone. Each time we enter into communion in one of our relationships, we gain the skills and abilities to recognize the potential for deep communication in other relationships. With this awareness we are able to shift from communication to communion. Our desire is to align our actions with our intent, while being aware of opportunities to enter into the space of communion.

Within our relationship with self, we become more comfortable communicating at this level. We recognize that communion is possible only in an environment of silence. We explore ways to sustain our silence through contemplative and mindfulness practices. Regular periods of practice during the day anchor our awareness. To create the anchor points, incorporate at least three periods of mindfulness practice throughout the day. Our awareness created in those moments is more likely to continue during the spans between the anchor points.

In time the spans between the anchors are filled with aware-ness. As the spans between these anchor points of awareness are bridged, we are able to communicate deeply throughout the day. We notice opportunities for communion. I have found that incorporating at least three separate periods of formal contemplative practice into my daily routine creates anchor points for an environment of silence and awareness to grow throughout the day.

When we consciously rest in silence, we strengthen our quiet mind. Our awareness of distractions is increased. Communion em-powers us to navigate the minefield of distractions. Instead of obsess-ing on the distractions, we choose not to react to them. This movement away from distractions and toward response deepens intimacy in rela-tionship. Intimacy creates the fertile ground where communion occurs.

Once we have developed this practice of anchoring into aware-ness, our ability to perceive the extraordinary naturally increases. We have greater clarity. It becomes easier to be fully present, to identify distractions, and to respond compassionately. The intimacy of our rela-tionships is increased.

In times of engaged silence, our attention is drawn to an awareness of the Sacred. In the present moment, instead of reacting, we move confidently down the path of response. Communion becomes not only the preferred method of interaction; it also becomes a tool to deepen relationship.

Our life really is all about us and our responses to the world. Reactions mire us in illusion's bog. When we are unable to let go of our illusions, our fears overwhelm us. We are more likely to react defen-sively and from our judgments and assumptions. Our reactions fuel our judgments, assumptions, and defensive behavior. Our reactions create a cycle in which we are often unaware. Communion does not allow us to hide from our reactions.

In order to break this cycle, we enter into hyperawareness. Engaging in RI^2 helps us identify the reactions that mire us in illusion. We gain clarity through reflection and introspection and enact our learnings during integration. Each time we practice RI^2, we gain under-standing and act upon it. This is our task as we strive toward a life of communion.

In moments of clarity and awareness, we open our eyes to the extraordinary in the world and gain opportunities to share authentically who we are. Our authentic sharing has the potential to trigger real, honest sharing from others. This sharing comes from the core of their being and connects others to their authentic self. The arc of communion connects their authentic being with ours. This endless cycle is perpetuated through contemplative relationship.

Within this space of authentic sharing resides communion. In this safe place we are able to respond with humility and courage. Accessing our curious daring and injecting enthusiasm into our interactions create wide-open connections to our self, others, the Sacred, and all of creation. Communion becomes a two-way communication powered by full-body listening.

Communion may begin with our self, but through our relationships it spirals out to others. In this spiraling we have opportunities to create brief but intimate relationships with often unexpected sojourners. We have the potential to gather a community of diverse twinkling stars in our constellation of connections.

Creating a Constellation of Connections

Sit quietly. Focus on your breathing. Do not try to shift your breathing. Allow it to naturally flow in and out. Through your breath, enter the ground of your being. Connect with your core relationship—the one with your self.

Enter a state of hyperawareness. Engage in full-body listening using all your accessible senses.

Describe your relationship using all of your senses:

What does it look like?

What do you hear?

What are you feeling?

What do you taste?

What do you smell?

Being an objective observer and using the 4nons (non-attachment, nonjudgment, nondefensiveness, and nonviolence), notice your thoughts and emotions.

Using the information gathered, answer the following questions:

- How are you connected to your authentic being?
- What parts of your self are false or part of the illusion?
- Choose one illusion and through the process of RI^2 (reflection, introspection, and integration) and in communion, create a plan to release the illusion and rest more firmly in your authentic self.

Chapter 15

An Internal Conversation of Connectivity

The vastness of the night sky invites us into silence. Each star is a twinkling solitary island. With our relationships we connect the dots and form constellations. No longer alone, we experience the hum of community echoing throughout our being. Our inward silence creates a welcoming environment for our external relationships to flourish. Within the silence, we listen to our distractions and respond with compassion. The noise in our life is not lessened; rather, our body becomes fine-tuned by hyperawareness. We are better able to filter distractions.

Our distractions are clearly identified in this state of hyperawareness. Within the silence, the ramifications of our choices become evident. We can choose not to react to the distractions by responding in loving, gentle ways. As we respond, the sparks of our compassion flare. An arc of compassion connects our self to others intimately and intentionally. Fueled by full-body listening and compassionate response, we create communion. We pass beyond differences through respect, reach understanding in common ground, and become one.

We enter common ground with others and with all of creation through communion. Common ground is not a place of agreement; we work toward understanding through mutual respect. Birthed and nurtured in our essence, communion thrives in common ground. Our relationship with the Sacred thrives each time we enter communion. We connect to the Sacred through our divine spark. At the hub of any act of communion is our divine spark.

Imagine for a moment that our divine spark is like a Fourth of July sparkler. Once lit, the spark arcs, creating an effervescent halo. So it is with communion. In the silence, our divine spark flares across the abyss and connects with the Sacred in a wordless, intangible way. We create communion through traditional prayer and any time we dialogue with the Sacred. Communion is the connection between us, others, all of creation, and the world.

When the spark flares communion with our self, we are aware of our internal monologue. With this awareness, the conversation is no longer a nondirected smattering of thoughts. We become more aware of the roots of our internal monologue and gain clarity of our beliefs, judgments, and assumptions. Communion provides the filter that brings understanding and order to this internal conversation.

Resting in our quiet mind, we understand what lies at the root of our self talk. Through communion, we discover the reasons behind our reactions and responses. With courage, we release our hurts and begin to heal. Through communion we understand how we may be sabotaging our self; By filtering our negative self talk, our self-compassion deepens. We honestly access the best paths to authentic presence. And, in these moments, the night sky that had been three separate components forms the older unity that Thomas Merton speaks of: "We are already one. But we imagine that we are not. And what we have to recover is our original unity. What we have to be is what we are."[12]

Our night sky becomes a unified one. All parts form a cohesive whole. We integrate the knowing that we are never alone. Each moment presents opportunities for connection. A smile, a kind word, an acknowledgement of the other creates, if only in that moment, relationship. When we live from the place of this "older unity," no moment is wasted. We are less likely to let go an opportunity to connect to others in meaningful ways.

Communion with others and all of creation is not possible unless we practice some degree of communion with our self and the Sacred. Listening with our full bodies to others and the world around us is possible only when we are aware of our thoughts, judgments, and beliefs. We must be comfortable with listening to our internal monologue while dialoguing externally with others.

Communion is a venture in bi-listening. While we attend to what the other is saying, we are mindful of how we are being triggered by the interaction. We notice when our judgments and assumptions rise to a boiling point and threaten to erupt. We are also aware of our distractions and how they draw us away from the moment.

With this awareness comes power. We have the power to live in response. When we choose to give rein to our reactions, we break the fragile tendrils of communion. Instead, we choose our actions and words in ways that share compassion. Connections are strengthened. Without a quiet mind, we are unable to prevent the fractures in relationship. A quiet mind is instrumental to communion and contemplative relationship.

We cannot be reminded enough that within the silence of our quiet mind, our internal monologue germinates. When we befriend our internal monologue, we gain knowledge about our perception of the world. We are given information to use as we discern what is real and what is illusion. We gain awareness of our authentic self and identify the angst and fears that create our illusions.

Our internal monologue cannot be ignored or discounted. If we allow it to run amuck without censure, our world becomes mired in illusion. By shaping our internal monologue with courage, humility, and honesty, we form the vessel in which communion flows. Through this deep communication, we can further recognize the obstacles that prevent us from freely and fully engaging in relationship.

These obstacles revealed by our internal monologue are deeply embedded in the ground of our being. The thoughts whispered provide clues to our judgments and assumptions. When we courageously move beyond our thoughts deeper into the ground of our being, we are able to name beliefs, assumptions, and judgments. Communion with our self empowers us to navigate the maze of illusions. We comprehend how our beliefs and judgments are formed and strengthened. Then we are able to question their validity and get honest answers.

Discovering the truth or the illusion inherent in this monologue does not occur in our logical mind alone. Full-body listening is required. Through it, we use all of our senses. Using all our senses, we see patterns and inconsistencies within the monologue. For us to fully understand this information, the practice of RI^2 is helpful. RI^2 acts as a filter of reframing our experiences into ones that best reflect our authentic self.

Our body, mind, spirit, and emotions hold a wealth of information that we gain when we listen to them. We carry somatic memories in our body. These are gathered throughout our lifetime. Seeing one person may flood us with feelings of good will; we may find our self relaxing. Another person may fill us with fear as we find our body clenching. When we learn to recognize and interpret our body's responses and discover what triggers them, we gain opportunities to reach a new level of understanding. Our body does not lie to us. It intuitively responds. We have only to learn the language and translate what we are given.

I knew a man professionally who was outwardly warm, loving, and kind. Yet, every time I met with him, I cringed. All of my alarms were sounding. Internally, something shouted at me to run. One day I saw his profile of his face, and I was flooded with the realization that he reminded me of my ex-husband. Although this man was unlike my ex-husband on many levels, physically he was similar. And that similarity triggered my reaction. Once I recognized what was causing this visceral response, I was able to minimize the impact of the trigger. I no longer reacted to him with fear.

We seldom think of our interactions as tasting or smelling a particular way, but we listen unconsciously with our senses of taste and smell. While it is not uncommon to have an actual sensation of flavor, many times the words "that leaves a bad taste in my mouth" pop into our mind. Asking the question "What is unpalatable about this situation?" may return a surprising response. When words like this pop in your mind, check in with your mouth. What are you tasting?

"Something smells rotten" is another phrase we use. As with all somatic experiences, we reflect upon what is triggering the response.

By "reflect," I mean attending to what we are sensing without becoming attached, without judging, and without defending. The goal is to gain information about what is triggering a reaction and to understand why we react. Then we can shift our reactions to responses.

The information we receive from our two primary senses, sight and hearing, may be unacknowledged or the impact understated. We look but do not see. We hear but do not listen. Communion invites us into a different way of perceiving using our eyes and ears. We look and hear beyond the physical, mundane world and delve into the world of our heart. In this place we notice what the other is saying on a deep, wordless level. We respond at this level. We identify and celebrate the extraordinary.

In my studies as an intuitive healer, I have read many authors who don't believe in an additional or sixth sense. Barbara Ann Brennan refers to our ability to enter into this extraordinary knowing as a high sense perception. For example, when we are in the moment and practicing hyperawareness, our eyes may be drawn to something that is out of place, or we may receive a clue that life is not in balance. We use this knowledge to reach new levels of intimacy as we connect through communion.

Hyperawareness is not an additional sense. We do not have the fabled sixth sense. Rather, it is the optimal use of all our senses. When we respond to our hyperawareness, it is the ultimate filter. Our ability to access information through an individual sense may be heightened. Or we may find that all our senses combine to create this heightened awareness. Each of us can learn to cultivate hyperawareness and use it to deepen intimacy in our relationships.

Using the 4nons (nonattachment, nonjudgment, nondefensiveness, and nonviolence) while listening with our entire body creates hypersensitivity. We understand what is said less by actual words and more by the nuances and cadences of what is being said. We notice the language of the body. We connect with all of our senses and, through this connection, enter communion. With hyperawareness, this inner knowing is no longer just a nebulous feeling, but an awareness filled with clarity. At times we may understand "why we know what we know," while at other times we take this knowing on faith.

When the information bombardment intensifies, we quickly become desensitized to this overstimulation and overload of information. Our senses become dulled. We lose our fragile connection to the silence of our quiet mind. We may lose contact with our external connections. Resting in the silence and entering the state of hyperawareness creates filters for this information overload. Using these filters, we identify what is necessary and what provides distractions.

Creating and becoming competent in using the filters takes time and practice. Developing an environment of silence is a lifelong process in which we discover the pathways of our intuition. As we strengthen our ability to respond to our intuitive nudges, we facilitate and deepen our ability to engage communion in ways that help us achieve intimacy in relationships. Trust in our self is needed. Through practice and trust we forge a deeper connection, a deeper communion with our self. In time this connection transcends the barriers of self and stimulates intimacy in our other relationships.

The RI^2 process (reflection, introspection, and integration) is a helpful tool for discerning how to engage our hyperawareness through full-body listening. Each of us has a unique, full-body listening signature. Both reflection and introspection provide clues to our unique way of listening. With self-discovery, we discern how we listen with our entire being and how to practice engaging our hyperawareness.

Over time we find that it is easier to recognize and respond to our sensory cues. Through practice and awareness, our ability to engage full-body listening without conscious thought becomes second nature. Our connection to communion becomes flexible, permeable, and organic. Full-body listening invites us into greater awareness and deeper connection as it illuminates the path to common ground. While in common ground, we dialogue with others in increasingly more intimate ways.

Creating a Constellation of Connections

Sit quietly. Focus on your breathing. Do not try to shift your breathing. Allow it to naturally flow in and out. Through the inhale and exhale, visualize entering into the ground of your being.

Unless we have filters, we become inundated with information. Filters enable us to sift through the plethora of information and discern what is helpful and what is distracting. Filters are unique to each of us. Some work better for us than others. Filters have one thing in common: they activate through our awareness.

Focusing on your breath activates the filter through which information comes. With each breath be aware of how a conversation, a behavior, or any stimulus in the world around you washes over you. Use full-body listening. If helpful, engage in the RI^2 process of reflection, introspection, and integration.

Name the triggers of reaction. Filter those triggers that would cause reactions in you.

Using RI^2, name ways of moving from reaction to response. Integrate a new way of response.

Chapter 16

Reaching Common Ground

Partners in contemplative relationships communicate with communion. They reside in common ground. In this place, we grow the intimacy of connection through honesty, truth, courage, and understanding. Reaching common ground does not mean that we agree with another. This common ground is seeded with unconditional love and nourished with compassion. Within common ground we reach understanding through compassionate presence. We agree to respectfully understand.

Although we may disagree, we have a loving response for the other. We are empathetic and pose questions in nonjudgmental, nonviolent ways. Aware of our agendas, we choose not to push them. Rather, we are nonattached to any particular outcome. We are open to the natural, evolving nature of connection through contemplative relationship.

This place of common ground is created with our collective silence and nurtured by the practice of the 4nons (nonattachment, nonjudgment, nondefensiveness, and nonviolence). Collective silence is nurtured when each person in relationship lets go of personal agendas. As each listens with intent and responds with compassion, silence is birthed in the moments of pause. Within silence, we recognize our distractions and choose our responses. Conversations are learning experiences where jumping to conclusions is minimized.

Collective silence empowers the relationship's evolution. We enter into connections in which no one is invisible. We see each person as important and as a connection within the inky night sky of silence. By resting in silence, we become hyperaware and are better able to explore the illusions that impel us to reaction.

Without the 4nons we would be unable to sustain silence. Through them, we reach understanding and recognize our commonality. We agree to seek information that presents accurate portrayals of all viewpoints. We do not blindly attach to our opinions. We are aware of and agree to suspend our judgments. We take care not to react defensively. Violent thoughts, words, and actions are minimized. Our unwavering use of the 4nons invites others into this way of being present.

Creating and maintaining common ground begins with each of us, with an understanding of our true self. Our relationship with our self forms the foundation of all other relationships. If this relationship is strife with illusions and mistruths, we are unable to fully connect with our true self. Any relationship in which we engage mirrors our illusions. If I do not believe I am lovable, I may gravitate to relationships that "prove" this illusion.

The same is true when we are unable to let go of attachments and judgments. If we hold onto the perception that our way is the best or the only way, we are blind to the most beneficial path to intimacy. Through our authentic self, we discover extraordinary ways of connecting with the other. When we let go of our attachments and the need to steer the course of relationship, we connect contemplatively. The relationship truly is fluid and organic.

Continuous awareness of our internal monologue is key to connecting with another. Even when we are interacting with others, we are aware of what prevents us from deepening the connection. We enter into communion with our self in order to assess our willingness to fully connect. We identify what is hindering our movement toward communion with others.

Self-awareness is the anchor of all relationships. We continue to gather information and use our wisdom to evaluate how the interaction impacts us. Once we understand the forces behind our thoughts, words, and actions, we are able to soften our stance. When we are no longer defensive, our openness triggers shifts in others.

Individual transformations encourage collective understanding. We engage in communion; communion draws us into deeper relationships. These deeper relationships are catalysts for communion in others; we create community.

We may reach consensus and common ground through the seven Gifts of the Spirit: knowledge, understanding, wisdom, courage, right judgment, reverence, and wonder and awe. Although these gifts are traditionally a Christian concept found in the Bible, the gifts transcend religion and culture. Each gift is as secular as it is spiritual and can be used in any setting in which we are communicating at the level of communion.

All of our actions and words are based upon our interpretation of information. Communion demands that we ask questions and listen to the responses while using the 4nons, then repeating this cycle until we reach a place of understanding with both our self and the other. Once we reach clarity, we stand at the crossroads of choice. Here we choose to use our understanding as a means to gain common ground, to discuss compassionately, and to explain our position in healthy, nonviolent ways.

Wisdom asks us to honestly assess how we are using our understanding. Do we argue and justify our position and negate the position of another? Or do we use wisdom to gain insights into commonalities and use our understanding to build connection? With wisdom and courage, we move past the need of being right and the fear of being wrong. In this place, individual and collective wisdom sustains connection.

Courage requires awareness of self. To be courageous, we identify our fears and concerns and recognize how they prevent us from connecting intimately with others. With curious daring, we blaze the path of connection. When I morph into a stance of curiosity and dare myself to discover and live within the extraordinary, the path to common ground becomes visible. Curious daring is the energy behind courage and empowers us to make the best decision in the moment.

Being wise is possible only with humility. We accept that we are not the expert and may not have ideas and possible ways forward. When we live out of this knowing and listen to others, together we make right judgments. These right judgments or decisions are gained using the 4nons. Although we, as individuals, may be on different spiritual and/or secular paths, using the 4nons assists us in reaching common ground.

Within this safe place, we are more likely to note how our assumptions and judgments are hindering us. We are aware of defensive actions and any inwardly or outwardly focused violence. With this awareness comes the power of choice. We choose to move toward the good of the individual and the relationship. With this movement, we engage in thriving, contemplative relationship.

Using the first five gifts—knowledge, understanding, wisdom, courage, and right judgment—we begin the process of consensus building. Our internal and external worlds move into alignment. Consensus building requires that each of us understands our self. When we understand our judgments, assumptions, and motives, we make authentic decisions that positively impact our self, others, and even groups. Our authentic self is aware of illusions and comes prepared to create intimate connections based on the deepest level of respect, reverence.

When I was young, I often heard the phrase "respect your elders." As I grow older, respect flows to all as I acknowledge the opinions and stances of others. Reverence is a state of being that requires a deep or profound sharing of respect that connects one divine spark with another, even when we do not agree with the other. For me, reverence is key to successfully integrating each of the seven gifts during communion with our self, the Sacred, the other, and all of Creation.

We respect, but we do not blindly accept. A reverent stance brings us to a place of understanding without acting upon judgments, reacting defensively, or giving in to fear-fueled violence. By respecting the views of another, we may accomplish the seemingly impossible. We may find we have more in common with the other than we have differences.

The first six gifts—knowledge, understanding, wisdom, courage, right judgment, reverence—open the doors to live in awareness's abode. Being mindful in the moment allows us to move closer to consensus building. We see through the mundane into the extraordinary. With an awareness of the extraordinary nature of the world, we are filled with wonder and awe.

I ability to approach facts, live in wisdom, gain understanding, wrap our self in courage, make right judgments, and show reverence increases in frequency when we live in wonder and awe. In this place of possibility, the pettiness of life falls away. All that remains are the desire and the need to be in harmony.

Harmony is present when we engage with communion. A natural outcome of consciously practicing communion is taking a loving look at the real. Communion opens our quiet mind. We see with clarity the condition of our life. We no longer have the capacity to lie to our self. Through the seven gifts—knowledge, understanding, wisdom, courage, right judgment, reverence, and wonder and awe—and the 4nons—nonattachment, nonjudgment, nondefensiveness, and nonviolence—we release what is not working and transform our life. Communion is the path of transformation on which we open our self to greater connection, more intimate relationship, and closer community.

We shift our communications into a space of communion through the conscious dialogue that occurs in the silence of our quiet mind. We are aware of the organic, flexible nature of each connection. Instead of directing the dialogue, we listen with our full body to the cues and respond intentionally to them. The connection flourishes; the contemplative relationship evolves.

Conscious external dialogue cannot occur without an awareness of our internal monologue. Intentionally listening to our internal monologue renders information as to how we hinder communion or encourage it. When we enter into communion with our internal monologue, our being expands and our ability to engage in communion with others increases. Our fears and challenges do not disappear during communion; rather, through communion we reveal and acknowledge them. Peace and silence soothe, energize, and empower us to respond in communion. This deep communication deescalates in ways that calm.

Humility, honesty, and authenticity within our self pave the way of communion. All of our relationships originate with the relationship with self. In order to communicate effectively with others from our heart, we must be authentic in our relationship with self. When our interactions are based on our illusions, our ability to connect with the other in deep, lasting ways is diminished. Communion requires that we be open to seeing, recognizing, and understanding who we are—both the truth and the illusion. When we are authentic, our thoughts, words, and actions are honest, humble, and loving.

Honesty is nonviolent. When we are secure in who we are, our integrity requires us to share our truth in loving, compassionate ways. Honesty does not seek to harm. We identify our illusions in ways that uplift and reveal the truth. Our connections to another deepen. We create a safe space where all can be honest. In this space the seeds of communion flourish. Where there is trust, fear is diminished; courage is the guiding force.

We have many facets to our self. Some are more palatable than others. Humility asks us to accept our self as we are by searching for ways to release the illusions and become ever more authentic. We acknowledge that we are human but recognize that our life is fueled by our sacred spark. This spark shines the light on our authentic self while highlighting the parts that require transformation. This transformation does not occur in a bubble. Interactions with others help us identify what is a sham and what is truly ours.

I am often humbled when I read something that I have written or when someone reminds me of something that I have said. In those moments, I recognize that my words are greater than me. I have entered into communion not only with myself and others but also with the Sacred. My connections with others are humbling, for through them I recognize my authentic self and temper the reactionary parts of myself. Connecting with others brings me to a place of peace that is only possible within the silence of my quiet mind.

As with all contemplative practices, communion is a skill that is refined each time we engage it. Communion requires full-body listening. Using all of our senses, we place our emphasis on listening. Our response happens as a result of this intentional listening. When we listen without attachment and by suspending judgments, we hear what is said in a different way. In this awareness, common ground is possible.

By listening without forming our response while the other is speaking, we create the opportunity for the dialogue to continue without an agenda. Our conversation is organic. We do not direct the conversation; it evolves. We open our self to the possibility of understanding with compassion and entering into intimate relationship. This is possible only through the awareness of our internal monologue and external dialogue. We use both to enter common ground, which is possible through conscious dialogue.

Conscious dialogue requires bi-listening. We attend to what the other is saying through their body, mind, spirit, and heart. At the same time, we attend to our internal monologue while noticing how our beliefs, judgments, and assumptions guide the course of our interactions. Through this awareness, we enter into the rhythm of the conversation.

Our potential reactions are tempered. We respond compassionately. We realize that each reaction causes minute cracks in the connection. Each compassionate response repairs those connections. These responses are part of communion. By successfully listening to our internal monologue, we strengthen our ability to choose response instead of reaction. Communion is the result.

Communion calls our attention to being in two places at the same time. Outwardly, we listen with our heart. Inwardly, we practice self-compassion as we are ever mindful of how our thoughts impact our relationships. While we may never be totally comfortable with this bi-listening, in time we can and do develop a level of expertise. This ability is necessary to developing sustained communion.

Response and reaction are our two choices each time we interact with another. When our actions are based on our fears and are triggered by old hurts, we react. Our interactions are mired in illusion. Instead of peering beyond our perceptions to discover what is real, we cling to what is comfortable and comforting. The dense fog of illusion prevents us from becoming intimate.

Response is possible when we feel safe. We create this safety both internally and externally. When we feel secure, we step outside our comfort zone and dig through the muck to reach what lies in our authentic core. Through the silence in our quiet mind, we respond with our compassionate heart. Together, silence and compassion foster an environment in which communion flourishes.

Our divine sparks connect. We begin to consciously search for understanding. We reach deeper levels of intimacy in all our relationships, and communications become multidimensional. We recognize moments of synchronization and search for ways to recreate them. We reach deeper levels of intimacy in all our relationships. Our contemplative relationships propel us into the extraordinariness of the world.

Communion connects the divine sparks in our constellation. Through it we continue to deepen and maintain the silence. We awaken our awareness and deepen our understanding not only of our self but also of the authentic nature in those with whom we are in relationship.

Without silence we would be unable to see clearly the intensity with which our divine sparks glow. Within the silence we see the possibility of relationships with our self, others, the Sacred, and all creation. Within the silence we engage our quiet mind and reach out to the quiet minds of others. When our divine sparks connect, the mundane becomes the extraordinary.

We open the eyes of our soul and see the pathways of connection. We dance along these connections in wordless and word-filled ways. Communion is more than a means to connect to one another in relationship. It is the gateway to intimacy. As we pass beyond the superfluous, relationships become intimate in the place of common ground.

Creating a Constellation of Connections

Sit quietly. Focus on your breathing. Do not try to shift your breathing. Allow it to naturally flow in and out. Through your breath, enter the ground of your being.

Recall a time you entered common ground in a relationship and gained understanding.

Reflect upon how the seven Gifts of the Spirit (knowledge, understanding, wisdom, courage, right judgment, reverence, and wonder and awe) helped you gain common ground. How did they help you remain in communion?

Identify how you used each of the seven gifts to and gain understanding.

What "right judgment" did you discover?

How did it enable you to revere the other?

Reflect upon a time that you were unable to rest in common ground and reach understanding.

Which of the seven gifts (there may be more than one) prevented you from deepening your connection?

How might you have made better use of the seven gifts to come to a right judgment in ways that deeply respected the other?

Chapter 17

From Intentio to Actio

Each relationship is a triad of divine sparks. Two glowing embers serve to anchor each of our relationships: our own divine spark and the blazing fire of the Sacred, the Source of all. The third piece of the triad represents a person, group, or part of creation with which we have formed a connection. Flexible and organic, these connections may glow brightly at times and then ebb into the dimmest life. This depends upon the type of connections and the health of the relationship.

At the conception of our spirit and the spirit of all sentient beings, a piece of the Sacred is given to us. Through our divine spark we have an everlasting, secure connection to the Sacred. It is there even in those dark nights when we cannot fathom its connection. This relationship is the light that guides us to our authentic self.

No matter what other relationships we form, we always maintain our connection to the Source. The connection is accessed through the silence of our quiet mind. Through our relationship with the Sacred, our compassion engages. Our compassion flares across this connection with communion to ignite the spark of another.

Our connection with the Sacred is strengthened through awareness. The seeds of this awareness are scattered and take root each time we engage in a contemplative or mindfulness practice. In these moments we live in awareness of how our intent and action are connected. I have developed a way of aligning intent with action loosely based on the ancient Catholic contemplative practice of Lectio Divina.

From Latin, Lectio Divina is translated as sacred reading. It is used to deepen understanding of Sacred Scripture. The four-step process invites us to begin by reading the text or lectio. Next, we enter into a time of reflective awareness or meditatio. During meditatio or meditation, we notice what words, phrases, or images speak to us. The third part is oratio or prayer. The understanding we have received in meditation helps to form our prayer in oratio. Finally, we enter into a place of quiet listening or contemplation. Within contemplatio, we receive a greater understanding of the reading.

For me, living in awareness involves the final three steps of Lectio Divina—meditatio, oratio, and contemplatio—which are flanked by intentio (intent) and actio (action). The five steps—intentio, meditatio, oratio, contemplatio, and actio—are the guides through which we increase our awareness and live mindfully in the moment. Integrating this way of being empowers us as we are in relationship. The five steps from intentio to actio help us maintain an environment of silence in which the ember of our compassion blazes and is channeled to another through communion.

At first, while learning these steps, we may methodically follow them in order. As we become more comfortable, we integrate the rhythm of intentio to actio in whatever order needed. This practice becomes second nature. We intuitively engage the steps as needed in the moment. Moving from intent to action, we enter the silence, and our relationships move from mundane to extraordinary. The three components of our night sky—silence, compassion, and communion—create a richness of connection that begins with intentio.

Intentio

Each morning when we awake, we consciously or unconsciously set our intent for the day. We may consciously set our intent through prayer, meditation, or a morning ritual like drinking a cup of coffee while turning our thoughts toward our hopes for the day. This conscious forming of intent is likely to move us into a place of peace and calm resiliency. By consciously setting our intent, we are better able to respond compassionately to life's blips.

Unconsciously setting intent gives power to our worries or fears. We get busy, we are distracted, and we are drawn into the past or propelled into the future. Unaware, we set our intent. Instead of creating a mindful place of peace, we have created an inadvertent reactionary place filled with discord. We do not need to stay in this place filled with havoc. In any moment we may wake up and recognize that our intent is not in alignment with our authentic self. With this knowledge comes the power to shift our intent to channel our deep compassion into authentic relationship.

Anytime over the course of the day, intention can be reset, bringing the eye of consciousness back into alignment with your authentic self, the Sacred, and others. We reset our conscious intent through informal contemplative practices. These may be mindfully breathing for thirty seconds or a brief walk. Any activity that breaks through the monotony of the day and brings us into awareness provides opportunities for reset. Intentio propels us on the journey to communion.

Meditatio

Our intent (intentio) is deepened or reset by the practice of meditation (meditatio). Times of meditation allow us to focus our attention on the present and be aware of opportunities to enter into relationship.

In each moment during which we are mindfully present, we really notice on many levels. We listen to our internal monologue, siphon off the distractions, and reflect upon our response. This reflection may be instantaneous, and we act. Other times, we create a memory of what occurred and tuck it into our quiet mind. We can call upon this memory as a reflection point at a later time.

Through meditation our attention roots into the present moment. We engage in full-body listening and identify the gifts and challenges inherent in the moment. With meditation our roots grow deeper into the ground of our daily interactions. Those inter-actions may be internal and connected to our relationship with our self or with the Sacred, or they may be external and the result of our relationships with others or creation. Through these interactions and in meditation we begin to formulate our prayer or engage in oratio.

Oratio

Oratio is the active, self-directed part of our conversation with the Sacred. We formulate our petitions, show gratitude, or pre-pare requests for forgiveness. Oratio, for me, is more than conven-tional prayer. Thomas Merton reminds us that "our spiritual life is first of all a life."[13] I understand this to mean that our every thought, word, and action has the potential to be a prayer. In each moment we can choose to connect to the Sacred.

Prayer in every thought, word, and action may overwhelm us with a sense of responsibility. Reflect upon your day in order to discern which of your actions, thoughts, and words were authentic and true. This exercise is a lesson in honesty, courage, and humility. We may need to allow self-compassion to flow as we create new patterns of response and rescript our reactions.

If we are truly in the moment and aware of what is happen-ing, we realize immediately the effects of our words and actions on our self and others. By entering into meditatio we reflect. Oratio is the fashioning of compassionate response to our self and to others. Our intentio, coupled with meditatio, empowers our ability to re-spond. In each moment of oratio we assert our intent to engage the other in relationship.

Contemplatio

The first three steps are active and outward moving. Through these we consciously form the base of all our relationships. This base is seeded with what is true and accurate in our self. Con-templatio is an inward-focused state. During contemplatio we rest in the silence and listen to the responses to our thoughts, words, and actions. These responses are the result of our contemplatio. The answers to our prayers are revealed to us in many ways—a quiet knowing, the words of another, a happening in nature, song lyrics, words in print, or some other way. Since all is connected, contemplatio can occur at any time and in any of our core relationships. These core relationships are with our self, the Sacred, others, and all of creation.

Contemplatio requires that we engage in full-body listening through an awareness that the information is received through all of our senses. We listen to both internal monologue and external dialogue in order to hear a response. Instead of focusing solely on what a person is saying or what is occurring in the environment, we attend to how beliefs, judgments, and assumptions are impacting our choices. These are the roots of our responses and reactions. When we attend to the internal and external simultaneously, we root firmly in the present. While contemplatio may appear passive, it is not. Listening for an answer requires hyperawareness.

Practicing contemplatio helps us shift a behavior that is hurtful, harmful, inconsiderate, or unaware. Even if we are unable to articulate oratio, resting in the silence with the intent to listen for the answer is enough to manifest a response through contemplatio. When we receive the reply, we have the power to manifest it in actio. Over time I have become aware of the power behind my words. I have become a proponent of choosing the most nonviolent language. During a conversation when I am more in alignment with my internal monologue, contemplatio helps me choose the best words to represent my thoughts.

Actio

This stage is more than our physical actions. It encompasses all of our responses and reactions, including our thoughts and words. Throughout the day, with every breath, we act. At times our actions are responses made in full awareness of our intent. When the response grows out of our intent, we more deeply root in the moment through meditatio. These actions also reflect other aspects of this sacred conversation: oratio and contemplatio.

In other moments our actions are fear-induced reactions. We realize history cannot be re-written. We cannot change a previous reaction or alter the truth of a memory. We can use these moments as learning opportunities. When we recognize our actio as reactive, we revisit our intentio through meditatio. Our oratio may be two-fold. First, it is the statement of our desire to move from fear-filled reaction to compassionate response. Second, we affirm our intent. Through contemplatio, we listen with the ear of our heart.

When we are aware of our actions, we have a barometer to measure how we are manifesting our intent. When we find our self missing the mark, we return to meditatio, oratio, and contemplatio. Even focusing five minutes on these three steps, we gain the power to propel us into authentic living.

When we live in awareness, we strengthen the connection of all relationships. We better understand who we are, we can more easily identify what is true, and we recognize where our illusions are embedded. Being authentic requires honesty with our self. This honesty seeps into the whole of our lives, and each relationship is positively impacted.

These five steps are profound guides for the whole of our life. The steps require that we enter into a state of hyperawareness. When we attain this level of awareness, little is hidden. We live honestly and with integrity, for full-body listening does not allow us to lie to our self. Living our intent in each of our actions empowers us to burn through the fog of our illusions and to connect more deeply to who is waiting patiently beneath this fog. That being is our authentic self who connects with all compassionately while in communion. These are contemplative relationships that form our constellation of connections.

Creating a Constellation of Connections

Sit quietly. Focus on your breathing. Do not try to shift your breathing. Allow it to naturally flow in and out. Through your breath, enter the ground of your being. Using intentio to actio, set your intent for the day.

Intentio: Ask yourself what you desire for the day. Spend a few moments focusing on your breath. Use these moments to form your intent through your words and/or thoughts. Next, visualize your intent entering your being through your breath.

Meditatio: Turn your awareness to the Sacred. How is it inviting you to manifest your intent? What distractions are barring your intent? Bookmark these distractions. With awareness, intend to navigate around them.

Oratio: Return to your intent. Does it need to be rescripted or refined as a result of meditatio? (What distractions did you discover that may prevent you from aligning your intent with your action?) Restate your intent, knowing you may need to restate and tweak it throughout the day.

Contemplatio: Find a place just to be. Focus on your breathing. Listen to the whispers, your intuition, as they well up from your being. Again, you may need to tweak your intent or be called to act upon it.

Actio: Throughout the day, whenever you are aware, align your intent with your action. When you need to use the three steps to refocus, do so. The initial four steps are part of your action.

Chapter 18

Dynamic Constellation

We can read until our sight blurs or talk to another philosophically until our voice becomes hoarse, but the ultimate way to learn to be in contemplative relationship is through experience. Our experience is dynamic, flexible, and evolving. What we experience in each of our relationships is part of our life canvas. Each relationship has the potential to propel us into transformation or mire us in the status quo.

Whether or not we take advantage of the possibilities of transformation depends on our ability to identify and utilize the many gifts each relationship presents. These gifts may be loving and gentle. They may also be angst producing. Whatever the gifts package, we can be sure of the relationship's ability to encourage growth. When we are fully aware in the moment, we take advantage of these empowering gifts. We recognize these gifts through full-body listening.

Full-body listening is a multisensory way of connecting. Inwardly we become aware of our thoughts, beliefs, judgments, and emotions. Through this inward focus, we identify how both our authentic nature and our illusions impact the relationship with our self and others. We must understand what is true and what is illusory about our self. If we are not aware of the hows or whys about our self, we will forever be lost in the loop of our illusions, triggering reactions that fortify illusions.

Hyperawareness invites us to discover our triggers and the ways to intentionally avoid reacting to them. Through full-body listening, we connect to what the other is saying. Using all five of our senses, we notice the world. A conversation is no longer just words, inflections, and body gestures. With hyperawareness, we access the vibrant colors of communion with which to paint our life canvas. We acknowledge the power of contemplative relationship. With this power, we transform and evolve.

Intuitively, we may be drawn to something that seems inconsequential. When we acknowledge it, our world shifts, our compassion flows, our connections are strengthened. In doing so, we recognize its importance. We may describe the world with sentences beginning with "I see," "I sense," "I feel," and "It appears to me." Using the 4nons (nonattachment, nonjudgment, nondefensiveness, and nonviolence), we shift our response to the world. We objectively respond in ways that deepen our understanding of the experience.

Nonattachment means that, instead of clinging to what we believe is the right answer or the right way, we set aside our desire to be right. We consciously allow our self to be open to possibilities that manifest. Nonattachment gives us the space where we recognize the bubbles of awareness that continuously burst into our understanding. We let go of any agendas as we wait in eager anticipation for cues that will lead us to heartfelt relationship.

Being nonjudgmental does not mean we never have another judgmental thought. Those, I believe, are inevitable consequences of living. Rather, we are aware of those judgments. We choose not to be distracted by them. We do not use them as a basis for hurtful or violent behavior. Our judgments provide us with information that assists us in understanding our actions and shifting our reactions to responses. Practicing a nonjudgmental stance creates a safe place where common ground may be reached and communion initiated.

It is never easy to see what lies at the roots of disharmony in our relationships. It is often difficult not to become defensive, argue our position, or excuse our behavior. Being nondefensive requires courage and humility. Not only do we accept our humanness and imperfections, but we also use them courageously as impetus for radical change. Actions fueled by the humility to admit our mistakes and the courage to correct our behavior merge to create a roadmap of transformation. The streets on the map are paved with communion.

Violence comes in many forms and is often not the result of an overt word or action. The root of violence lies in our thoughts. In fact, if we are not following the first 3nons, nonattachment, nonjudgment, and nondefensiveness, we are likely to exhibit violent behavior. The root of all violence is intangible—based upon our beliefs, judgments, and assumptions. Violence begins when the silence in our quiet mind is disturbed by our distractions. Unchecked, it manifests in our reactions.

Living in a state of hyperawareness, we minimize the potential of reaction. In those moments during which we are forced backward into the past or propelled into the future, our beliefs, judgments, and assumptions may bypass our compassion barriers and burst forth violently in our words and actions. Being mindfully aware minimizes our step into another time or another place. In the moment, we reduce the chance of violence.

When we agree to be nonviolent, we agree to be vigilant about the subtle and pervasive violence that lurks in our quiet mind. These subtle forms of violence can be eradicated through challenging our judgments and assumptions in the moments that they occur. As we become comfortable with the stance of the objective observer, we intuitively use all 4nons — nonattachment, nonjudgment, nondefensiveness, nonviolence.

Full-body listening is an important, necessary component of contemplative relationship. Relationships shift and change. We cannot discern our role in a relationship or the relationship's role in our life without full-body listening. It is the gateway to communion. I remember recognizing how distracted I was during a conversation with a client. When I shifted to full-body listening, I was no longer driving the conversation with my agenda. Instead, the conversation evolved into a beautiful sharing. Without my responses based upon cues received from full-body listening, she might not have reached her understanding.

Full-body listening is an important component of hyper-awareness. Through hyperawareness, we recognize the beneficial and potentially harmful impact a relationship has on our life. Truthfully identifying and accepting the other's impact on each of our lives begins the process of each partner's growth. There are no "bad guys" in contemplative relationships; rather, these relationships and the partners within are vehicles for growth and transformation.

Answering the following questions may give us information to use during discernment. Honest and, at times, painful answers lead to a greater understanding of our role in the relationship and our beliefs about what we need and want in the relationship. Remember to use full-body listening as you answer these questions. Don't just document thoughts, but describe emotions or any intangible unsettled feelings. Also include any joy-filled or uplifting aspects of the relationship.

The questions:

- How do I want to be in this relationship?
- What do I need from my partner?
- How do I receive what I want and need?
- How do I perceive that the other wants to be in relationship with me?
- How able am I to provide what that person needs?

These questions are answered not as islands but as integral to deepening relationship in intimacy. You may want to encourage your partner to answer the same questions. Our responses provide talking points for an honest, compassionate conversation with the other in relationship. When necessary, engage a third party such as a counselor or mediator to help bring clarity to your responses.

After each conversation with the other, a period of personal reflection follows. As individuals, each of you should begin the process of discerning your abilities to be in the relationship in supportive, life-giving ways. Then discern what, in your opinion, needs to shift in order to maintain the integrity of the relationship. Create an image of how this change will look. This visualization is limited only by your judgments and assumptions.

The relationship may deepen and become more profound and integral to your life, or it may be less intertwined with your life and gravitate away from its center. Neither is better or worse, right or wrong. Relationships ebb and flow over time to meet our needs and the needs of those in relationship with us. Resting in the common ground helps us answer these questions, understand the potential of the relationship, and allow it to naturally evolve.

This discernment process is not engaged lightly. It cannot be accomplished in five minutes. Working toward balance and alignment in a relationship is difficult. Discernment is a process that guides the way to common ground and life-giving relationships. Each partner must be invested in using discernment as a way of resolving issues and strengthening the relationships.

Always remember that the process of discernment begins with the self. If our relationship with our self is balanced and authentic, our other relationships will mirror that balance. To create relationships, we must be honest, courageous, and humble. The goal of any relationship is transformation of the self and others in ways that will bring greater alignment with our life purpose.

No matter what relationship we are discerning, the process impacts our relationship with our self and our relationship with the Sacred. The results of discernment in one relationship will likely impact our relationship with self and relationships with others. Growing a more authentic relationship with our self impacts our relationships with others; authentic relationships with others impact our relationship with self. Authenticity shines the light on illusions and provides resources to bring greater harmony to relationships.

Through discernment we engage more fully in relationship. RI^2 (reflection, introspection, and integration) is a beneficial component of discernment. In reflection we objectively refocus our attention, during introspection we reframe our understanding, and during integration we respond. While we may acknowledge that we are fearful of deep reflection or the change discernment will bring, courageously we gather facts necessary to our introspection. Courage is present when we find patterns and truth in our behavior. Through integration we create a new way of interacting. The elements of our night sky synchronize. Silence, compassion, and communion unite.

When we experience silence with our self and others, distractions become more visible. Through self-compassion, we navigate our internal mine fields. Sharing compassion with others neutralizes our desire to battle. By infusing our lives with compassion, we naturally and intuitively cause no harm and alleviate suffering. Through compassion and silence, we form fibers that twine together to make the connection of communion. Like the sky on a clear night, our constellation of connections twinkles brightly as a beacon of our most authentic self.

Creating a Constellation of Connections

Sit quietly. Focus on your breathing. Do not try to shift your breathing. Allow it to naturally flow in and out. Through your breath, enter the ground of your being. Choose a relationship to use for this exercise.

Reflect upon the relationship. Answer the following questions using full-body listening and hyperawareness. Notice how your body is responding. Explore its reactions with all of your senses to obtain a greater understanding. Attend to your thoughts and judgments. With hyperawareness, what do you notice? Is there something spiritual, mental, emotional, or physical that either resonates with you or brings you dissonance? Listen with your body, mind, spirit, and heart as you discern:

- How do I want to be in this relationship?
- What do I need from my partner?
- How do I receive what I want and need?

- How do I perceive that the other wants to be in relationship with me?
- How able am I to provide what that person needs?

The answers to these questions can help you gain awareness about whether the relationship needs to shift and how to best shift it into a more intimate connection.

Afterword

Living in a city with the night sky diminished by light pollution, I often yearn for a clear, sparkling sky filled with constellations. Even though I am unable to physically see the constellations, I have found a way to create my own unique skyscape. The sky twinkles with constellations of connections, my relationships and the relationships of others.

At many times over the course of writing this book, I took consolation in the understanding that relationships are dynamic, evolving, and transformative. There are many opportunities to "get it right," "try again," or "just let go" in loving, compassion-filled ways. Relationship has become the vehicle through which I live my life and touch others in phenomenal ways. My relationship partners nudge me closer to my authentic self.

What is the most surprising thing that I learned on this journey? My life really is all about me. How I shed my illusions and transform into my most authentic self is the foundation of my life path. How I respond or react in my relationships are the steps along the path. This transformation is possible only through forgiveness, unconditional love, and compassion.

Just as important, I have learned that your life is really all about you. I have heard the phrase "it is not all about you" often. I disagree. Our responses or reactions to each action, every word, and all thoughts are about the ways we choose to live in the world. So life really is about us. We cannot prevent another's hurtful actions or words, but we can choose a loving, generous response instead of a domino-effect reaction. The most loving, compassionate response may be to leave a situation.

As a partner in relationship, each of us is both a student and a teacher. Our greatest classrooms are our relationships. With awareness, we accept the lesson. Through full-body listening, we learn the lessons. In each moment of relationship, the opportunities of joy and happiness exist. Relationship is what propels us through our life. I hope that you and I and all others can live fully, unconditionally, and compassionately in our constellations of connections.

Finally, it seems that this life, for all of us, is really about relationship. My hope, my dream, my wish for each of us is that we relish the messiness inherent in relationship, that we use the three parts of our night sky to connect, learn, grow, love, and be in glorious relationship. When it is time to let go of a relationship, may it happen with integrity, forgiveness, and compassion. Most of all, I hope that we find, in each relationship, nuggets of truth that will spark awareness and empower each of us to live in gloriously intentional and compassion-filled ways.

Vanessa F. Hurst
Mother's Day 2016

Works Cited

[1] Thomas Merton, Thoughts in Solitude (New York: Farrar, Strauss, Giroux, 1956), #.

[2] Benedict of Nursia, A Reader's Version of The Rule of Saint Benedict in Inclusive Language (Erie, PA: Benedictine Sisters of Erie, Inc., 1989), #.

[3] Benedict of Nursia, A Reader's Version of The Rule of Saint Benedict in Inclusive Language, #.

[4] Naomi Burton, Patrick Hart, and James Laughlin, eds., The Asian Journal of Thomas Merton (New York: New Directions, 1973), #.

[5] David A. Cooper, God Is a Verb. (New York: Riverhead Books, 1997), #.

[6] Pema Chödrön, Comfortable with Uncertainty (Boston: Shambhala Press, 2003), 123.

[7] Thomas Merton, Raids on the Unspeakable (New York: New Directions, 1966), 15.

[8] R. E. Daggy, ed., Honorable Reader: Reflections on My Work (New York: Crossroads, 1985), 123.

[9] Patrick Hart and Jonathan Montaldo, eds., The Intimate Merton: His Life from His Journals (New York: HarperCollins, 1999), 327.

[10] Naomi Burton, Patrick Hart, and James Laughlin, eds., The Asian Journal of Thomas Merton (New York: New Directions, 1973), 308.

[11] Burton, Hart, and Laughlin, The Asian Journal of Thomas Merton, 308.

[12] Burton, Hart, and Laughlin, The Asian Journal of Thomas Merton, 308

[13] Merton, Thoughts in Solitude, 37.

Biography

Vanessa F. Hurst reminds herself that, "she hasn't failed; she can tell herself 10,000 ways not to be in relationship." She believes that the best way to connect is through contemplative relationship. Vanessa is ever grateful for the compassion shown by her partners in relationship including her son Merlin, G.G., Peggy, Ivan, and all those intimate strangers. For her, developing and sustaining contemplative relationships happens through awareness and practice.

Holding a master's degree in Natural Health, Vanessa is an Intuitive Coach. Sharing her intuitive vision, she empowers clients to engage their inner wisdom in ways that lead to more mindful living. Vanessa understands that living contemplatively and compassionately is the root to healing the woundedness in our self and the world. She believes that life is best experienced holistically through our body, mind, spirit, and heart (emotions).

As a Compassion Consultant, she facilitates organizational queries that lead to the identification of compassion in their cultures and the development of strategies for strengthening elements of compassion and creating new avenues of compassionate action.

She facilitates programs on compassion, contemplative living, mindful awareness, and intuitive awareness. The signature of these programs is holistic experiences that engage the body, mind, spirit, and heart of participants.

Contact Vanessa at hurst.vanessa@gmail.com
For more information: www.intentandaction.com